Skinny Louisiana
. . . in the Kitchen

Skinny Louisiana . . . in the Kitchen

Shelly Marie Redmond, MS, RD, LDN

Foreword by Marlyn Monette

PELICAN PUBLISHING COMPANY

GRETNA 2017

First printing, February 2017
Second printing, May 2017

Library of Congress Cataloging-in-Publication Data

Names: Redmond, Shelly Marie, author.
Title: Skinny Louisiana . . . in the kitchen / Shelly Marie Redmond, MS, RD,
    LDN, Culinary Dietitian ; foreword by Marlyn Monette.
Description: Gretna, Louisiana : Pelican Publishing Company, Inc., 2017. |
    Includes index.
Identifiers: LCCN 2016033712| ISBN 9781455622719 (pbk. : alk. paper) | ISBN
    9781455622726 (e-book)
Subjects: LCSH: Cooking, Cajun. | Cooking, Creole—Louisiana style. | Low-fat
    diet—Recipes. | LCGFT: Cookbooks.
Classification: LCC TX715.2.L68 R43 2017 | DDC 641.59763—dc23 LC record available at
https://lccn.loc.gov/2016033712

Printed in the United States of America

Published by Pelican Publishing Company, Inc.
1000 Burmaster Street, Gretna, Louisiana 70053

To Edna and Louise, my two grandmothers

CONTENTS

ForeWord

I, like Shelly Redmond, hail from South Louisiana, so you can imagine my excitement to find a kindred spirit move in and take Shreveport by storm with her enthusiasm and cooking expertise! As a cookbook author, food writer, and former caterer, I'm delighted to claim Shelly as an invaluable resource and a great friend. She has added zest to my life and taught me that one never stops learning!

Shelly's "skinny" food creations, as well as her bright wit and enthusiasm, draw people like a magnet, and she is in demand as a guest speaker, where she never fails to put a spark in her audience as she teaches them about smart food choices. I wouldn't miss her monthly "Cooking with the Dietitian" classes, where she captures her audience's attention while dispensing a hearty dose of smart cooking tips, followed by a sampling of her delicious cuisine.

At last, we have this exciting new book, *Skinny Louisiana . . . in the Kitchen*, to enjoy in our home kitchens. This book is a fun read, and Shelly's simple recipes, tips, and advice will have you clamoring for more. She is indeed an inspiration, and her *joie de vivre* (joy of living) is contagious. Enjoy!

Marlyn Monette
Author of *So Good . . . Make You Slap Your Mama!* and
So Good . . . Make You Slap Your Mama! II

PreFace

It seems as though every time we turn on the local news in this fantastic state, we see a very important person, wearing a white lab coat, talking about health in Louisiana. Their name is proudly monogrammed on their lab coat, followed by tons of initials. Their attitude is quite angry, and they state with a scowl, "Louisiana is one of the top-five fattest states in the country."

I'll give them credit where credit is due. In the latest *The State of Obesity: Better Policies for a Healthier America*, Louisiana's adult obesity rate was at 34.9 percent. This is up from 22.6 percent in 2000 and 12.3 percent in 1990. But what the important person with tons of initials behind their name says next is a mistake: "We are fat because the food in this state is fattening. Quit eating it." I have the facts to prove this wrong.

Is our food really fattening? Quite the contrary: Louisiana is a top producer of foods that are great for our health. Louisiana pecans are a rich source of omega-3, Louisiana sweet potatoes are an amazing source of vitamin A, and boiled and grilled Louisiana seafood is a wonderful lean source of protein.

The problem is *not* the food of Louisiana. The problem is we are brainwashed into believing that our food is fattening, and as a result, many of us walk away from the amazing and healthy foods this state offers. Instead, we opt to follow the American habits of preparing fatty foods, visiting fast-food restaurants, and consuming large portions.

Am I saying we can have the foods our grandparents served? We can have our jambalaya and shrimp? Yes, I am saying that we can.

You may be asking yourself what makes me the expert on this topic and why you should listen. I was born in Houma, Louisiana into a family that celebrates our Cajun heritage. When someone is born, we celebrate; when someone gets married, we really celebrate; and when someone dies, we celebrate them into the ground. Yes, our celebrations always revolved around food. But the food came from this state, including boiled crawfish, wild game, okra, beans, and tomatoes. We never went to fast-food restaurants, and we ate what we grew. I had rabbits and a garden, and this led to my involvement in 4-H. At the age of twelve, I was crowned Lafourche Parish Reserve Champion in my first cooking contest.

I realized then how much I loved food and how food makes people around me happy. As a result, I decided to major in food. I would graduate from both Nicholls State University and Louisiana Tech University with bachelor's and master's degrees in nutrition. I was ready to take over the world with food, until I had a rude awaking. . . .

I was so excited to walk into my first day's work at the VA Medical Center in Shreveport and start educating individuals about food. But I was greeted by disheartened patients, terrified I would tell them to eat plain baked chicken and steamed green beans. Many no-showed or didn't want to see the dietitian. How could this be? Why didn't patients want to talk to me?

As I walked around the clinic, I would hear this statement from many healthcare providers: "If it tastes good, spit it out." The brainwashing begins. Out of fear, the patient skips seeing me and returns three months later to the clinic heavier and more frustrated. Did that suggestion work? No!

The traditional eating plan that we tell individuals of bland chicken, tasteless salads, and cardboard rice cakes is a joke. I had to convince folks that the advice we gave them for years is a complete crock. It was difficult, but I was up for the challenge.

During this time, my love for food blossomed in the most unique fashion. A cute blond guy with glasses walked into my office and offered me a brownie. "Looks like you need this," he said and quickly walked out. My mood changed, and that brownie changed my life in more ways than one. I found the mysterious cute blond guy, and he told me a patient gave him the brownies as a thank-you. Then and there, I was reminded how food is used to thank others and show gratitude.

I decided right then that the answer to my challenge was to get folks excited about food. I went back to my roots, cooked more, and shared the dishes with my patients. The excitement spread beyond our patients to the general public. I was asked to go on local news stations to demonstrate how simple it is to cook healthy foods. I cooked instead of scolded, giving folks the line, "Oh my goodness, I can't believe it is that easy and yummy." The demonstrations were well received, and to this day I have TV segments on KTBS, KTAL, and KMSS in Shreveport. Magazines and companies took notice of how we were bringing delicious food back into our diets. *Men's Fitness* and *SELF* magazines as well as BuzzFeed featured my recipes.

In 2013, I opened my own private practice, where I work with individuals to bring favorite foods back into their lives with a skinny twist. We share laughter and recipes, and we cry happy tears when the numbers go down on the scale.

They are always amazed at how they can enjoy the dishes Maw Maw used to prepare and still lose weight. Need proof? My patients average a weight loss of four to ten pounds in the first month of working with me.

I discovered the secret. Food has to taste good, be pantry-friendly, and always represent our culture. You won't find any strange ingredients in my recipes, and my goal is to complement your life, not complicate it.

To start this lifestyle, as I do with all my clients, we must build our pantry and shop with the Skinny Louisiana mindset. My first chapters do just that. You will find tricks you can use to make your own recipes skinny, the exact products you should have in your pantry and kitchen, and what to look for on the food labels.

I then feature gorgeous, tasty recipes. Looking at these, you may panic at the sight of sugar, flour, or oil as ingredients, but my goal is to reduce these amounts by one-third—not fully eliminate them from the dish. The reason? I want to keep the flavor as authentic as possible. My intern, Britney Tracy, provided the nutritional facts for my skinny creations (calories, fats, sodium, carbohydrates, and sugars) as well as the traditional dishes, for comparison.

You will not see another cookbook of this kind. Sure, you many find healthy Louisiana recipes made with loads of artificial sweeteners, fat-free cheese, or gluten-free pasta, but I can bet they taste terrible or nothing like what you had on the table growing up.

If you want to celebrate life, enjoy food, and live life with a skinny twist, this book is for you. I challenge you to bring Louisiana back to your table. I will show you how easy and tasty it is to celebrate Louisiana living and cooking . . . with a skinny twist!

Oh, and the brownie guy? I married him.

Let's bring on the skinny!

ACKNOWLEDGMENTS

This book would not have been possible without the support and love of amazing people in my life. Thank you from the bottom of my heart to . . .

The wonderful doctors, nurses, and personal trainers in Shreveport and Bossier City who refer their patients to my clinic. Thank you for trusting me to guide your patients on a path to improved health and fitness.

My clients. Your stories inspire me. You don't realize the impact you have had on my life. Thank you for your honesty, the tears we cried, and the happy dances we shared in my office. You inspire me to be better and to reach for my goals.

My media family. Thank you for allowing me to haul my cooking equipment to your stations for our segments. Thanks for being awesome taste testers and posing for fabulous pictures with the food.

My fabulous dietitian colleagues, Cindy, Robin, Kate, Mitzi, Rebecca, Mary M., Amber, Abby, Jon, and Christy. Your love and support means so much.

My best friends, Susan, Brianna, and Hajii. Thank you for serving as a sounding board for all my personal and business ideas. Friends like you are hard to find, and I am blessed to say I have three.

My Cajun family. Thank you for loving me for who I am and never expecting me to change. Thank you for loving my fun Yankee husband and teaching him about our fabulous food and way of life.

Nena and Pawan. Thank you for defining unconditional love and letting me grow in your hearts.

My children, Mireille and Christian. Thank you for giving me your honest opinions about my food.

My Yankee husband, Greg. Thank you for offering me a brownie that morning when we worked together at the VA Medical Center in Shreveport. You knew that the best way to my heart was through food, and we haven't looked back since. Thank you for embracing the Cajun life as your own.

Skinny Louisiana
. . . in the Kitchen

The Skinny Louisiana Pantry

A well-stocked pantry is the cornerstone of *Skinny Louisiana . . . in the Kitchen.* Simple and healthy modifications to your Louisiana-based recipes can be made with the following ingredients, and I use many of these items in the dishes presented here. Be sure to stock your pantry with these ingredients, to start your Skinny Louisiana lifestyle.

Mission Carb Balance Wraps. These high-fiber wraps are incredibly low in net carbohydrates. Available in small, medium, and large sizes, the medium wrap adds only 6 grams of net carbohydrates to a meal. This product can be found in the bread section of many Louisiana supermarkets.

Flatout Flatbread. Who doesn't love pizza? I use this fun product as a pizza crust in the Skinny Louisiana kitchen due to its high fiber count. Flatout makes a variety of flavors, so just make sure to pick up the ones with 5 grams of fiber or higher.

Fiber Gourmet Pasta. This product is incredibly high in fiber and low in net carbohydrates (only 20 grams of net carbohydrates per ½ cup, as compared to 35 grams of net carbohydrates in traditional whole-grain pasta). The downside? Only a few Louisiana stores carry this pasta. But don't worry; you can order it online.

Panko breadcrumbs. Who would have guessed there is such a huge difference of carbohydrates in the varieties of breadcrumbs? Panko breadcrumbs contain almost ½ the carbohydrates of regular breadcrumbs (24 grams compared to 40 grams of carbohydrates per ½ cup). My favorite brand is Kikkoman.

Beans. Don't wait till Mondays to serve these. Beans are an incredible source of fiber, yielding between 5 and 7 grams per ½ cup. They make great add-ins to chilis, soups, and sauces. Need more motivation? White beans contain our weight-loss weapon: resistant starch. Resistant starch resists digestion and feeds our healthy bacteria, thus keeping us fuller longer.

Sweet potatoes. Our state vegetable, the sweet potato is a nutrition powerhouse. One medium sweet potato is only 130 calories but boasts 4 grams of fiber. When eaten cold, they are a wonderful source of resistant starch.

Canola oil. This monounsaturated oil serves as a great replacement for butter in many of my savory or sweet recipes. In fact, you can use a smaller amount of this oil than butter and save calories in the process.

Peanut oil. While many of our grandparents used peanut oil for frying, think of it instead as great for sautéing meat. Peanut oil is high in a monounsaturated fat called oleic acid, which can help reduce appetite. Need more convincing? Research from the University of California, Irvine found that this oil can boost memory.

Tabasco pepper sauce varieties. Many individuals run from hot sauce, thinking it is high in sodium. I am thrilled to announce I use it in the Skinny Louisiana kitchen, with my favorite being Tabasco. The reason? Tabasco uses vinegar and aged peppers, so it is very low in sodium. One teaspoon yields only 35 milligrams of sodium, making this product perfect for a low-sodium diet plan.

Cajun/Creole seasoning. Did you know you were saving sodium by using Cajun or Creole seasoning? Substituting it for salt in all my recipes cuts the sodium by $\frac{1}{2}$. The Skinny Louisiana kitchen is stocked with Tony Chachere's Creole Lite Seasoning as well as Chef Paul Prudhomme's Magic Seasoning Blends, including Lemon & Cracked Pepper, Seven Herb, Sweet & Spicy, Toasted Onion & Garlic, and Six Spice.

Fiber One Cereal (Original). This is a must-have in any Skinny Louisiana kitchen. At only 60 calories and packed with 14 grams of fiber per $\frac{1}{2}$ cup serving, it not only makes a great breakfast choice, but it also is a wonderful add-in to many of my favorite recipes. Crushed Fiber One drastically reduces the net carbohydrate count of my recipes due to its high fiber count. Use in your own recipes by replacing $\frac{1}{2}$ of your all-purpose flour or breadcrumbs with crushed Fiber One.

All-Bran Bran Buds Cereal. This is another winner, with only 80 calories but 13 grams of fiber in a $\frac{1}{3}$ cup serving. In addition to a good breakfast, All-Bran cereal is a wonderful partial substitution in dessert bars. Punch up the fiber by replacing $\frac{1}{2}$ of the all-purpose flour with All-Bran Bran Buds.

Rolled oats. Like Fiber One and All-Bran, rolled oats make a great breakfast staple. At only 120 calories but with 4 grams of fiber per $\frac{1}{2}$ cup serving, they serve as a healthy partial substitution for flour in dessert bars. In addition, rolled oats are a weight-loss powerhouse since they contain resistant starch. Replace $\frac{1}{2}$ of the all-purpose flour in your own bar recipes with rolled oats.

Almond flour. While almond flour is one of the pricier items in my pantry, it makes an incredible partial substitution for all-purpose flour in my cupcakes. Don't be alarmed by the fat in this product—this gluten-free flour contains only

6 grams of carbohydrates but 3 grams of fiber per ¼ cup. Substitutions are a little tricky with almond flour, so follow the package directions for best results.

Graham crackers. We think of graham crackers as a quick snack, but in the Skinny Louisiana kitchen, I use them as a crust for my pies and in other desserts. The reason? A traditional piecrust can have 800 calories, 48 grams of fat, and 96 grams of carbohydrates, while one made of 1 cup crushed graham crackers and 1 tbsp. canola oil yields only 479 calories, 22 grams of fat, and 64 grams of carbohydrates.

Pecans. Louisiana pecans are a weight-loss and health winner. These yummy nuts star in many of my dessert recipes. Not only are pecans a beloved Louisiana product, but a recent study from Loma Linda University in California revealed that when they are part of a daily diet, levels of bad cholesterol in the blood are lowered. Need a little more motivation? Just 1 ounce of pecans provides 10 percent of the daily recommended intake of fiber.

Applesauce. This makes an incredible partial substitute for both sugar and butter in my dessert recipes. By replacing ½ cup sugar with ½ cup applesauce, I am slashing 304 calories and 78 grams of carbohydrates. For even more savings, use unsweetened applesauce in your recipes. Simply replace ½ the sugar and/or ½ the butter with applesauce in any of your desserts for a delicious lower-carb, lower-calorie result.

Marshmallow fluff. The difference in calories and carbohydrates between marshmallow fluff and sugar is incredible. By using marshmallow fluff in place of sugar in some of my sweet dips, I am saving 56 calories and 15 grams of carbohydrates per 2 tablespoons. When you make this substitution in your own recipes and add 1 tsp. vanilla extract, your guests will not miss the sugar.

Vanilla extract. This is the star flavoring in many of my dessert recipes. If you are removing ½ cup sugar from the dish, add 1 tsp. vanilla extract.

Skinny Louisiana Kitchen Necessities

In addition to stocking your pantry, supply your kitchen with yummy refrigerated and frozen goods and helpful equipment, to start your Skinny Louisiana lifestyle.

ReFrigerated aNd FrozeN GoodS

Greek yogurt. The Skinny Louisiana refrigerator is always stocked with plain Greek yogurt. It makes an amazing substitute for sour cream and mayonnaise in dip recipes, heavy cream in pasta recipes, and butter in dessert recipes. Plain Greek yogurt adds a double punch of protein and calcium without the extra fat and calories of those other ingredients. To compare, ½ cup Greek yogurt contains 150 calories and 4 grams of fat, while ½ cup butter contains 814 calories and 92 grams of fat. Simply replace ½ of the sour cream, mayonnaise, cream, or butter in your personal recipes with Greek yogurt. For example, if a recipe calls for 1 cup mayonnaise, use ½ cup plain Greek yogurt and ½ cup mayonnaise.

Light cream cheese. I love cream cheese, but I am always conscious of how I can cut calories without cutting nutrients. Light cream cheese is prepared with skim milk, thus reducing the calorie count without increasing carbohydrates or sugar. Need more convincing? One tablespoon of light cream cheese is 30 calories, compared to 1 tbsp. regular cream cheese at 40 calories. While the 10 calorie savings seems small, trust me—calories add up quickly!

2 percent milk. Milk is an important staple in the Skinny Louisiana kitchen. For those who don't want to switch to skim milk (only 80 calories per 1 cup), use 2 percent milk instead of whole milk in recipes. It will save you 30 calories without losing any essential nutrients (including calcium) and protein that whole milk provides.

Although the research is emerging, there are new studies showing there is no strong evidence that saturated fat in dairy foods is associated with an increased risk of heart disease. However, as it only has 120 calories per cup, you can confidently enjoy 2 percent milk, as long as you balance total calories. Individuals concerned about carbohydrates in milk can select Fairlife milk. Since Fairlife is ultra-filtrated, it yields half the carbohydrates and sugar of regular milk and is great for the diabetic population.

Half-and-half. While many use this in coffee, it is a great replacement for heavy cream in many of my pasta and dessert recipes. One half-cup of half-and-half contains 161 calories, 13 grams of fat, and 4.8 grams of carbohydrates, while ½ cup heavy cream contains 400 calories, 40 grams of fat, and 3 grams of carbohydrates.

Plain sparkling water. While I love a cocktail, I don't love the calories! Use plain sparkling water in your cocktail recipes to increase the "bubbly" without increasing the calorie count.

Eggs. Did you know eggs are an amazing source of both protein and choline, a nutrient needed for brain health? I never replace them in my recipes. I embrace the health benefits of eggs. A large egg contains only 75 calories but packs 6 grams of protein. And yes, my cholesterol is normal!

Frozen shrimp. This Louisiana seafood superstar packs an amazing amount of protein in comparison to its low calorie count. Taking only 5 to 7 minutes to sauté on the stovetop (cook until opaque), this easy-to-cook protein powerhouse contains less than 100 calories and 18 grams of protein per 3-oz. serving.

Frozen vegetables. Open up a Skinny Louisiana freezer, and you will find an array of frozen vegetables. From simple steam-in-the-bag varieties to seasoning mixes for soups and gumbos, they take minutes off cooking and side-dish preparation. While steam-in-the-bag varieties are great for busy evenings, experiment with roasting frozen vegetables instead. My vegetables chapter contains some yummy examples. Purchase varieties with 5 grams of sugar or less.

Equipment

Rolling pin. Does this sound old-fashioned? Well, a rolling pin is essential for crushing Fiber One Cereal and panko breadcrumbs for use in many of my recipes.

Food processor. Save money by processing rolled oats or Fiber One into flour.

Electric hand mixer. While I love a standing mixer, an electric hand mixer will suffice for all of my dessert recipes.

Various mixing bowls. Save money by shopping local flea markets, country stores, and online outlets.

Various nonstick pots and pans. Some of my best nonstick pots and pans have been purchased at garage sales or passed down to me from my aunts.

Parchment paper. For my dessert recipes, I always line my baking pans with parchment paper to prevent foods from sticking. Look for this product in the foil or food-storage section of your local supermarket.

SKINNY LOUISIANA at the Grocery Store

While I love to grocery shop, I know that many folks are not the biggest fans of spending time at crowded, loud supermarkets. Old-school nutrition ideas teach us to only shop the perimeter of the store, but we now know that this area can stock products high in fat, calories, sodium, and carbs, while the inner aisles can carry incredibly healthy items low in fat and high in fiber. What is the secret to mastering the supermarket? Follow my plan below.

Set a consistent date and time. I encourage each of my clients to stick to a shopping routine. Many have found that Thursday or Friday evenings are a great time to go, since the stores seem to be less hectic and crowded than on the weekend.

Make a list. Once you set a time in your planner, it is vital to develop a shopping list. Without one, we tend to both overbuy and forget essential products.

Check prices at wholesale clubs. Nonperishable items can often be purchased there in bulk. Some wholesale clubs will even allow you to order online and pick up at the store. This saves not only time but money.

Start shopping the aisles. As I stated, we tend to skip the aisles for fear of purchasing products high in calories, fat, sodium, and carbs. But aisles contain grains, cereals, beans, marinades, spices, and rubs.

Focus on fiber. Be sure to read the labels and purchase products with 5 grams of fiber or higher. Fiber is a weight-loss weapon in that it keeps us fuller longer. Also, note that fiber contains *0* calories, so the higher a product is in fiber, the lower its calorie count.

Load up on frozen vegetables. By stocking up on steam-in-the-bag frozen vegetables, you can have a side dish at your table in 5 minutes. Cauliflower is a particularly good choice, since you can substitute it for some of the carbs in many of my dishes.

Limit sugar. Focus on products with 5 grams of sugar or less.

Hit the dairy and meat sections on the perimeter. Fill your cart with the following protein-rich items: Greek yogurt, 2 percent milk, reduced-fat cheese, sirloin, chicken, pork loin, and shrimp.

Finish with fruits and vegetables. Save fruits and vegetables for last, to prevent them from being damaged or bruised from the weight of other products. Look for fruits higher in fiber, including berries, apples, and pears, as well as longer-lasting vegetables such as green beans, cabbage, broccoli, and cauliflower. Add our Louisiana trinity of onions, bell peppers, and celery, and finish with our superfood, the sweet potato.

Sauces, Dressings, and Dips

ROCK-'N'-ROLL REMOULADE SAUCE

While remoulade sauce is commonly served with shrimp, I love using the skinny version as a dip for boiled crawfish and shrimp as well as a spread for lunch wraps. Traditionally, this sauce is heavily mayonnaise based, so I "skinny-ed" it simply by using plain Greek yogurt. It not only saves calories and fat but also increases the protein in the dish. Why does this matter? Protein is a key component in weight loss by promoting satiety, the feeling of fullness!

½ cup light mayonnaise
½ cup plain nonfat Greek yogurt
1½ tbsp. mustard
1 tsp. ketchup
1 tbsp. lemon juice
1 tbsp. Worcestershire sauce

½ cup minced onion
¼ cup parsley, minced
1 stalk celery, minced
½ tsp. paprika
1 tsp. Tabasco sauce

In a medium bowl, whisk together all ingredients. Cover and chill until ready to serve.

Yield: About 1½ cups

Serving Size: 2 tbsp.

Nutrition Facts per Serving
Calories: 60, Fat calories: 35, Total fat: 4 g, Saturated fat: 0.5 g, Cholesterol: less than 5 mg, Sodium: 135 mg, Total carbohydrates: 3 g, Dietary fiber: 0 g, Sugar: 2 g, Protein: 2 g

Traditional Remoulade Sauce Nutrition Facts per Serving
Calories: 143, Total fat: 15 g, Sodium: 213 mg, Total carbohydrates: 2 g, Sugar: 1 g

RaViSHiNG RaNCH DreSSiNG

Ranch-dressing lovers, rejoice! I have a very simple, skinny version you can use as a dip, dressing, or spread on your wraps. Ranch dressings and dips contain large amounts of fat due to the use of sour cream or mayonnaise. The skinny change? I replaced the mayonnaise with plain Greek yogurt, slashing calories and fat while increasing the protein and calcium content.

1 cup plain nonfat Greek yogurt
2 tbsp. ranch seasoning mix

In a medium bowl, whisk together ingredients. Chill until ready to serve.

Yield: 1 cup

Serving Size: 2 tbsp.

Nutrition Facts per Serving
Calories: 25, Fat calories: 0, Total fat, 0 g, Saturated fat: 0 g, Cholesterol: 0 g, Sodium: 190 mg, Total carbohydrates: 3 g, Dietary fiber: 0 g, Sugar: less than 1 g, Protein: 3 g

Traditional Ranch Dressing Nutrition Facts per Serving
Calories: 140, Total fat: 14 g, Sodium: 230 mg, Total carbohydrates: 2 g, Sugar: 1 g

I Can't Believe It's Creamy Italian Dressing

Say goodbye to tasteless, fat-free Italian dressing and say hello to this creamy, tasty version. As with my Ravishing Ranch Dressing, I skinny-ed this recipe by using plain Greek yogurt in place of sour cream or mayonnaise. Bottle this dressing for your daily salads or as a dip for raw vegetables.

1 cup plain nonfat Greek yogurt
2 tbsp. dry Italian dressing mix

In a medium bowl, whisk together ingredients. Chill until ready to serve.

Yield: 1 cup

Serving Size: 2 tbsp.

Nutrition Facts per Serving
Calories: 20, Fat calories: 0, Total fat: 0 g, Saturated fat: 0 g, Cholesterol: 0 mg, Sodium: 180 mg, Total carbohydrates: 2 g, Dietary fiber: 0 g, Sugar: 2 g, Protein: 3 g

Traditional Creamy Italian Dressing Nutrition Facts per Serving
Calories: 120, Total fat: 13 g, Sodium: 470 mg, Total carbohydrates: 3 g, Sugar: 2 g

WOW! ONiON DiP

Calling all sports fans! Makeover your chips and dip platter with this tasty dip. I followed my skinny strategy by replacing the sour cream and mayonnaise with plain nonfat Greek yogurt. Serve this dip with Shelly's Skinny Chips (see index), and your guests will be saying, "Oh, wow!"

1 cup plain nonfat Greek yogurt
2 tbsp. onion dip mix

In a medium bowl, whisk together ingredients. Chill until ready to serve.

Yield: 1 cup

Serving Size: 2 tbsp.

Nutrition Facts per Serving
Calories: 20, Fat calories: 0, Total fat: 0 g, Saturated fat: 0 g, Cholesterol: 0 g, Sodium: 160 mg, Total carbohydrates: 2 g, Dietary fiber: 0 g, Sugar: 1 g, Protein: 3 g

Traditional Onion Dip Nutrition Facts per Serving
Calories: 60, Total fat: 5 g, Sodium: 230 mg, Total carbohydrates: 2 g

DRINKS

Skinny Strawberry-Pomegranate Mimosa

Think that mimosas are only orange juice and champagne? Think again. This mimosa showcases the Louisiana strawberry and antioxidant-rich pomegranate juice. The skinny comes from using diet ginger ale as part of the liquid.

8 strawberries, sliced
6 oz. pomegranate juice

6 oz. champagne
6 oz. diet ginger ale

Divide strawberries among glasses. Pour equal parts pomegranate juice, champagne, and diet ginger ale into each glass. Serve.

Yield: 4 servings

Nutrition Facts per Serving
Calories: 60, Fat calories: 0, Total fat: 0 g, Saturated fat: 0 g, Cholesterol: 0 mg, Sodium: 20 mg, Total carbohydrates: 7 g, Dietary fiber: 0 g, Sugar: 6 g, Protein: 0 g

Traditional Mimosa Nutrition Facts per Serving
Calories: 92, Total fat: 0 g, Sodium: 5 mg, Total carbohydrates: 23 g, Sugar: 16 g

Skinny Louisiana Sunrise Mimosa

From a simple brunch to a holiday celebration, mimosas are incredibly popular. I love to add a Louisiana twist by using satsumas and strawberries. The skinny part? I reduce calories by replacing some of the champagne and juice with diet ginger ale.

1 satsuma, sliced
4 strawberries, halved lengthwise
6 oz. champagne

6 oz. light orange juice
6 oz. diet ginger ale

Divide satsumas and strawberries among glasses. Pour equal parts champagne, orange juice, and ginger ale into each glass. Serve.

Yield: 4 servings

Nutrition Facts per Serving
Calories: 60, Fat calories: 0, Total fat: 0 g, Saturated fat: 0 g, Cholesterol: 0 mg, Sodium: 20 mg, Total carbohydrates: 7 g, Dietary fiber: 0 g, Sugar: 6 g, Protein: 0 g

Traditional Mimosa Nutrition Facts per Serving
Calories: 92, Total fat: 0 g, Sodium: 5 mg, Total carbohydrates: 23 g, Sugar: 16 g

Divine Skinny Sangria

Nothing welcomes the gorgeous spring weather better than a sangria, but what we don't want to welcome is the high-calorie and sugar content of this popular and tasty beverage. The skinny solution comes from a simple addition and subtraction in the original recipe. I added diet ginger ale and subtracted from the amount of orange juice, thus reducing calories and sugar. The ginger ale adds a sparkling touch, making this drink a sure hit at your next event!

1 bottle red wine, chilled
4 oz. light orange juice
2 oranges, thinly sliced
2 lemons, thinly sliced

2 limes, thinly sliced
2 apples, cut into ½-inch chunks
16 oz. diet ginger ale

In a large punch bowl, combine red wine and orange juice. Add oranges, lemons, limes, and apples. Stir.

Add diet ginger ale. Stir. Serve.

Yield: 10 servings

Nutrition Facts per Serving
Calories: 60, Fat calories: 0, Total fat: 0 g, Saturated fat: 0 g, Cholesterol: 0 mg, Sodium: 15 mg, Total carbohydrates: 3 g, Dietary fiber: 0 g, Sugar 1 g, Protein: 0 g

Traditional Sangria Nutrition Facts per Serving
Calories: 142, Total fat: 0 g, Sodium: 9 mg, Total carbohydrates: 17 g, Sugar: 15.1 g

Appetizers

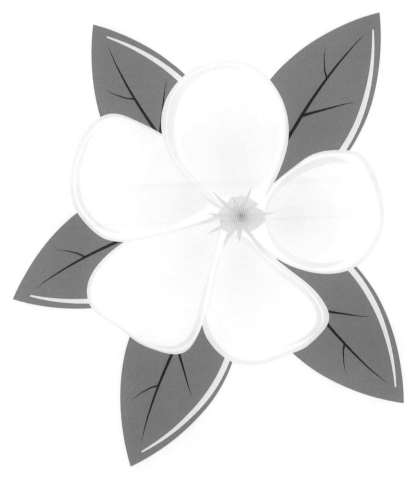

Baked 'N' Great Beet Chips

These gorgeous, purple-hued, low-carb, baked beet chips make a great snack at Mardi Gras celebrations. I know, beets seem a little . . . different. But trust me, this dish is a favorite at my food demonstrations. How do I know this? The tray is always empty when I clean up.

2 beets, rinsed and peeled

1 tbsp. olive oil

Pinch of salt

Pinch of black pepper

Preheat oven to 400 degrees. Line a baking sheet with parchment paper or aluminum foil.

Using a mandoline or sharp knife, thinly slice beets. (The thinner you slice, the crispier the beets will be.) Place sliced beets in a bowl.

Add olive oil, salt, and black pepper. Toss. Arrange beets in a single layer on baking sheet.

Bake for 15 minutes. Remove from oven. Toss.

Return to oven and bake an additional 10-15 minutes or until beets are crisp, checking at 5-minute intervals. Remove from oven and serve.

Yield: 4 servings

Nutrition Facts per Serving
Calories: 45, Fat calories: 27, Total fat: 3 g, Saturated fat: 1.5 g, Cholesterol: 0 mg, Sodium: 70 mg, Total carbohydrates: 4 g, Dietary fiber: 1 g, Protein: 1 g

Traditional Potato Chips Nutrition Facts per Serving
Calories: 160, Total fat: 10 g, Sodium: 170 mg, Total carbohydrates: 15 g

SHeLLy'S SKiNNy CHipS

Sadly, I have to share a bit of bad news. Traditional potato chips are not only loaded with fat and calories, but they also lack the fiber our bodies need. Shelly's Skinny Chips are the solution to your chip cravings. Made with Mission Carb Balance Tortillas, these chips are not only crispy and flavorful but also packed with fiber. They will soon replace your store-bought potato chips.

2 large Mission Carb Balance Tortillas
Nonstick cooking spray

Preheat oven to 450 degrees. Line a baking sheet with parchment paper or aluminum foil.

Cut each tortilla evenly into 8 wedges. Spray triangles with nonstick cooking spray. Place on baking sheet.

Bake for 3 minutes. Remove from oven and flip chips over on baking sheet. Return to oven and bake an additional 3 minutes. Remove from oven and serve.

Yield: 2 servings

Serving Size: 8 chips

Nutrition Facts per Serving
Calories: 120, Fat calories: 27, Total fat: 3 g, Saturated fat: 1.5 g, Cholesterol: 0 mg, Sodium: 300 mg, Total carbohydrates: 19.5 g, Dietary fiber: 15 g, Sugar: 0 g, Protein: 4.5 g

Traditional Potato Chips Nutrition Facts per Serving
Calories: 160, Total fat: 10 g, Sodium: 170 mg, Total carbohydrates: 15 g

"I Can't Believe It's Baked" Sweet Potato Chips

Nothing tastes better than a handful of chips. But fried chips are high in calories, fat, and sodium. This recipe is the answer to my chip obsession. Baking sweet potatoes drastically reduces the fat content, and combining light Cajun seasoning with a dash of salt creates a dish worthy of our vitamin-A-rich state vegetable. The result is a 90-calorie, gluten-free, low-saturated-fat chip for all my sweet-potato lovers!

2 medium sweet potatoes, scrubbed and peeled
¼ tsp. light Cajun seasoning

1 tsp. cinnamon
⅛ tsp. salt
1 tbsp. olive oil

Preheat oven to 450 degrees. Line 2 baking sheets with parchment paper or aluminum foil.

Using a mandoline, slice sweet potatoes and place in a bowl. Add Cajun seasoning, cinnamon, and salt. Toss.

Pour olive oil on top of sweet potatoes. Toss. Spread sweet potatoes evenly on both baking sheets, making sure slices do not touch each other.

Bake for 10 minutes. Remove from oven and toss. Return to oven and bake for 5-10 minutes or until sweet potatoes are crispy. Remove and serve.

Yield: 4 servings

Nutrition Facts per Serving
Calories: 90, Fat calories: 30, Total fat: 3.5 g, Saturated fat: 0 g, Cholesterol: 0 mg, Sodium: 150 mg, Total carbohydrates: 15 g, Dietary fiber: 3 g, Sugar: 3 g, Protein: 1 g

Traditional Potato Chips Nutrition Facts per Serving
Calories: 160, Total fat: 10 g, Sodium: 170 mg, Total carbohydrates: 15 g

Celebration Skinny Hot Crawfish Dip

I firmly believe we have five seasons in Louisiana— summer, fall, winter, spring, and crawfish! Crawfish season embodies the Skinny Louisiana motto: Louisiana living and cooking with a skinny twist. Crawfish boils are a part of life here, and ounce for ounce, these protein-rich crustaceans have fewer calories than chicken. In this dip, I replace full-fat cream cheese with a light variety, and I add a Louisiana flair with a bit of light Cajun seasoning. I serve it with high-fiber crackers or Shelly's Skinny Chips. This six-ingredient, low-carb, protein-rich, hot crawfish dip is sure to please your entire crowd!

2 tbsp. butter
1 green or yellow bell pepper, diced
2 cups spinach
1 tsp. light Cajun seasoning

1 lb. frozen cooked crawfish, thawed and drained
8 oz. ⅓-fat cream cheese
Fiber Gourmet crackers or Shelly's Skinny Chips

In a saucepan, melt butter over medium heat. Add bell pepper and cook for 5 minutes. Add spinach and seasoning. Cook for an additional 3 minutes.

Stir in the crawfish and cook for 8-10 minutes. Reduce heat to low and add cream cheese. Stir until cream cheese melts. Serve with high-fiber crackers or Shelly's Skinny Chips.

Yield: 8 servings

Nutrition Facts per Serving (dip only)
Calories: 130, Fat calories: 70, Total fat: 8 g, Saturated fat: 5 g, Cholesterol: 95 mg, Sodium: 350 mg, Total carbohydrates: 1 g, Dietary fiber: 0 g, Sugar: less than 1 g, Protein: 12 g

Creole 'N' Thin Hot Crab Dip

Available from our own waters, crab offers an amazing source of protein for our diets. In addition to the low calories provided by the crab, I skinny-ed this dip by using light cream cheese and shredded reduced-fat cheese. The result is a perfect appetizer for a chilly date night in or colder Mardi Gras celebrations. As always, serve with Shelly's Skinny Chips.

Nonstick cooking spray
2 8-oz. pkg. light cream cheese, softened
½ cup shredded reduced-fat cheddar cheese
2 tbsp. spicy mustard
2 tsp. Worcestershire sauce

¼ tsp. light Cajun seasoning
1 lb. or 2 6-oz. cans crabmeat, drained and
  picked through
1 onion, minced

Preheat oven to 350 degrees. Spray a 1-qt. casserole dish with nonstick cooking spray.

Combine remaining ingredients in a large bowl. Pour crab mixture into casserole dish. Bake for 30-35 minutes. Remove from oven and serve.

Yield: 20 servings

Nutrition Facts per Serving
Calories: 70, Fat calories: 40, Total fat: 4.5 g, Saturated fat: 4.5 g, Cholesterol: 0 mg, Sodium: 160 mg, Total carbohydrates: 3 g, Dietary fiber: 0 g, Sugar: 2 g, Protein: 4 g

Razzle, Dazzle, and Slim Red Bean Dip

Red beans and rice, a Louisiana staple traditionally served on Mondays, offer a wonderful source of fiber and protein for our diets. I love this dish and custom so much, I proudly wear a red-bean charm on a necklace. This dip embraces the Skinny Louisiana motto by celebrating our Monday culinary tradition and cutting down the total fat by using light cream cheese and shredded reduced-fat cheese. Is it complicated? Not at all. A simple food processor is all you need to dazzle the crowd. Serve with high-fiber crackers or Shelly's Skinny Chips, and say hello to your new Monday culinary tradition.

1 can red kidney beans, drained and rinsed
1 cup salsa

2 8-oz. pkg. light cream cheese, softened
1 cup shredded reduced-fat cheddar cheese

Place all ingredients in a food processor. Process until smooth and serve.

Yield: 24 servings

Serving Size: 2 tbsp.

Nutrition Facts per Serving
Calories: 70, Fat calories: 40, Total fat: 4.5 g, Saturated fat: 2.5 g, Cholesterol: 15 mg, Sodium: 200 mg, Total carbohydrates: 5 g, Dietary fiber: less than 1 g, Sugar: 2 g, Protein: 4 g

Marvelously Skinny Hot Muffuletta Dip

A spin on the traditional muffuletta, this dip is the perfect addition to any tailgating or Mardi Gras celebration. Every New Orleans guidebook calls this Italian sandwich a must-have culinary treat for visitors to enjoy before leaving town. The traditional muffuletta presents two nutritional challenges: a lot of sodium and a lot of carbs. After a careful review of the ingredients, I found I could skinny the dish and enjoy it in dip form by halving the salami, substituting both low-sodium ham and low-sodium olives, and eliminating the bread. The result is simply amazing—just ask my Yankee husband! As always, serve this warm, creamy dish with Shelly's Skinny Chips.

Nonstick cooking spray
8 oz. pkg. light cream cheese, softened
4 slices salami, diced
1 cup diced low-sodium ham
2-4-oz. can black olives, drained and sliced
1 6-oz. jar low-sodium green olives, drained and sliced

¾ cup roasted red peppers, drained and chopped
½ cup pickled peppers, drained and chopped
¼ cup chopped provolone cheese
½ cup shredded mozzarella cheese

Preheat oven to 350 degrees. Spray a 9x9-inch casserole dish with nonstick cooking spray.

Combine remaining ingredients in a bowl. Pour mixture into casserole dish. Bake for 25 minutes or until mixture is bubbling. Remove from oven and serve.

Yield: **20 servings**

Nutrition Facts per Serving
Calories: 100, Fat calories: 60, Total fat: 7 g, Saturated fat: 3 g, Cholesterol: 20 mg, Sodium: 420 mg, Total carbohydrates: 2 g, Dietary fiber: 0 g, Sugar: 1 g, Protein: 7 g

Traditional Muffuletta Nutrition Facts per Serving
Calories: 360, Total fat: 12 g, Sodium: 1,280 mg, Total carbohydrates: 64 g

Jazzy and Slim Hot Pepper Jelly Dip

How many of us have a jar of hot pepper jelly given as a Christmas present or bought from the local farmer's market? When I travel throughout this amazing state, one of my favorite souvenirs is locally prepared hot pepper jelly. Most varieties have around 8 grams of sugar per tablespoon. While this seems like a high amount (and we do want to be very conscious of our sugar and carb grams), we can still enjoy these jellies with a skinny twist. Enter my Jazzy and Slim Hot Pepper Jelly Dip. Similar recipes exist, but many use the entire jar of jelly. This skinny version calls for only ¼ cup. You still get the great taste of the jelly without all that sugar. Serve it with Shelly's Skinny Chips.

8 oz. ⅓-fat cream cheese, softened
¼ cup hot pepper jelly (such as blueberry)

Combine ingredients and serve.

Yield: *About 1 cup*

Serving Size: *2 tbsp.*

Nutrition Facts per Serving
Total carbohydrates: 3-4 g

Spectacular Skinny Crab-Stuffed Mushrooms

These mushrooms are tasty, gorgeous, a good source of fiber, and full of . . . crab. Seafood is the perfect Skinny Louisiana protein, and crabmeat is an especially amazing source for so few calories. A 3-oz. serving is approximately 65 calories while offering over 14 grams of protein. Crab stars in these stuffed mushrooms, and I continue the skinny twist with another secret—Fiber One Cereal! Traditionally, stuffed mushrooms are loaded with breadcrumbs (hello, carbs), but here I swap those out for crushed Fiber One Cereal and panko breadcrumbs. While this appetizer can get a little messy, it tastes so good it's worth it.

Nonstick cooking spray
1 cup crabmeat
4 oz. light cream cheese, softened
½ cup parsley, chopped
½ onion, chopped
¼ cup grated low-fat Parmesan cheese

¼ cup shredded low-fat mozzarella cheese
½ tsp. light Cajun seasoning
⅛ cup panko breadcrumbs (such as Kikkoman)
⅛ cup crushed Fiber One Cereal (Original)
4 portobello mushrooms, stems removed

Preheat oven to 375 degrees. Spray a baking sheet with nonstick cooking spray.

Combine crabmeat, light cream cheese, parsley, onion, Parmesan, mozzarella cheese, Cajun seasoning, panko breadcrumbs, and Fiber One.

Place mushrooms upside down on baking sheet. Spoon mixture onto mushrooms.

Bake for 15-20 minutes. Remove from oven and serve.

Yield: *4 servings*

Nutrition Facts per Serving
Calories: 140, Fat calories: 60, Total fat: 6 g, Saturated fat: 3.5 g, Cholesterol: 55 mg, Sodium: 580 mg, Total carbohydrates: 11 g, Dietary fiber: 3 g, Sugar: 5 g, Protein: 12 g

Traditional Crab-Stuffed Mushroom Nutrition Facts per Serving
Calories: 218, Total fat: 7 g, Sodium: 727 mg, Total carbohydrates: 29 g

SKiNNy SHriMp CoCKtaiL

This is the ultimate Skinny Louisiana appetizer! The gorgeous crowd pleaser features the amazing Louisiana shrimp. The shrimp packs a huge amount of protein in comparison to its low calorie count. As gorgeous as this dish is, it requires very little preparation. I skinny-ed the marinade by reducing the oil and adding flavorful lemon and lime juice. For the cocktail sauce, I decreased the chili sauce, thus lowering the carbs and sugar, and added lycopene-rich tomato juice.

10-16 oz. medium shrimp, cooked, peeled,
  and deveined

MARINADE
¼ cup olive oil
½ cup lime juice
¼ cup lemon juice
¼ cup minced red onion
6 lemon wedges
2 tbsp. minced parsley
Dash of salt
¼ tsp. Tabasco sauce

COCKTAIL SAUCE
¼ cup chili sauce
¼ cup tomato juice
2 tbsp. lemon juice
1 tbsp. prepared horseradish
1 tbsp. Worcestershire sauce
⅛ tsp. light Cajun seasoning

In a bowl, combine shrimp with all marinade ingredients. Cover and chill for 2-4 hours.

Meanwhile, in a small bowl, combine all sauce ingredients. Chill.

Remove shrimp from refrigerator and drain juices. Set lemon wedges aside. Spoon shrimp mixture into martini glasses. Garnish with lemon wedges. Serve with sauce.

Yield: 6 servings

Nutrition Facts per Serving
Calories: 160, Fat calories: 90, Total fat: 10 g, Saturated fat: 1.5 g, Cholesterol: 95 mg, Sodium: 530 mg, Total carbohydrates: 8 g, Dietary fiber: 0 g, Sugar: 2 g, Protein: 12 g

Slimmed-Down Crawfish Bread

Say hello to amazing flavor and goodbye to carbs when preparing this classic appetizer with high-fiber wraps. This dish has it all—looks, taste, and a Louisiana protein superstar, crawfish. I skinny-ed this appetizer by replacing heavy cream with plain Greek yogurt as well as using reduced-fat mozzarella and Parmesan cheese. While you can choose either French bread or Mission Carb Balance Wraps, diabetics should go with the wraps for lower carbs. Either way, I promise you won't be able to tell the difference between my skinny version and the restaurant version of this dish. This appetizer is so good that I showcased a shrimp variation in a Southeast Dairy Council online commercial.

Nonstick cooking spray
1 tbsp. olive oil
1 lb. crawfish tails, peeled and deveined
1 pt. cherry tomatoes, sliced
1½ tsp. light Cajun seasoning
1 cup shredded low-fat mozzarella cheese

¼ cup grated reduced-fat Parmesan cheese
½ cup plain nonfat Greek yogurt
¼ cup parsley, chopped
1 loaf French bread or 4 large Mission Carb Balance Wraps

Preheat oven to 350 degrees. Spray a baking sheet with nonstick cooking spray.

Set a skillet over medium heat. Add olive oil. Add crawfish, tomatoes, and Cajun seasoning. Sauté for 2 minutes. Remove from heat.

In a large bowl, combine cheeses, Greek yogurt, and parsley. Mix crawfish mixture into cheese mixture. Set aside.

Cut loaf in half crosswise, then lengthwise, or cut each Mission Carb Balance Wrap into 8 wedges. Place bread (cut side up) or wedges on baking sheet. Spoon crawfish mixture onto bread or wedges.

Bake for 10-15 minutes. Remove from oven. If using bread, cut into 2-inch sections. Serve.

Yield: 8-10 servings

Serving Size: 1 bread slice, or 4 Mission Carb wedges

Nutrition Facts per Serving (French bread)
Calories: 190, Fat calories: 45, Total fat: 5 g, Saturated fat: 2 g, Cholesterol: 70 mg, Sodium: 530 mg, Total carbohydrates: 20 g, Dietary fiber: 1 g, Sugar: 2 g, Protein: 17 g

Nutrition Facts per Serving (Mission Carb Balance Wraps)
Calories: 130, Fat calories: 45, Total fat: 5 g, Saturated fat: 2 g, Cholesterol: 70 mg, Sodium: 420 mg,
Total carbohydrates: 6 g, Dietary fiber: 3 g, Sugar: less than 1 g, Protein: 14 g

DaSHiNg 'N' THiN DeviLed Eggs

These low-carb deviled eggs contain a big secret: Greek yogurt. This skinny version will be your go-to appetizer for all your formal entertaining events. Eggs have gotten a bad rap, but they are a huge part of the Skinny Louisiana lifestyle. They are an amazing source of protein, keeping us feeling fuller longer, as well as choline, which is needed for healthy brain function. I also love supporting our state farmers and purchasing eggs straight from a local producer. I skinny-ed the traditional recipe by replacing ½ the mayonnaise with plain Greek yogurt. It lends an amazing thickness to the filling but with less fat. Watch in wonder as these eggs fly off your dinner table.

12 eggs, hard boiled, cooled, and peeled
¼ cup + 2 tbsp. plain Greek yogurt
¼ cup + 2 tbsp. light mayonnaise
1 tbsp. spicy mustard

1 tsp. light Cajun seasoning
Dash of salt
⅛ tsp. black pepper
Paprika (for garnish)

Cut eggs in half lengthwise. Place egg yolks in medium bowl. Set egg whites aside.

To egg yolks, add Greek yogurt, light mayonnaise, spicy mustard, light Cajun seasoning, salt, and pepper. Combine well. Fill each egg white with 1 tsp. egg-yolk mixture.

Sprinkle paprika on top. Place in refrigerator until ready to serve.

Yield: 12 servings

Serving Size: 2 halves

Nutrition Facts per Serving
Calories: 100, Fat calories: 70, Total fat: 7 g, Saturated fat: 2 g, Cholesterol: 190 mg, Sodium: 150 mg, Total carbohydrates: 1 g, Dietary fiber: 0 g, Sugar: 1 g, Protein: 7 g

Traditional Deviled Eggs Nutrition Facts per Serving
Calories: 262, Total fat: 8 g, Sodium: 150 mg

JUMPIN' SLIM JALAPEÑO HUSHPUPPIES

I love asking my friends and Skinny Louisiana social-media followers, "What dish do you want to see skinny-ed?" A repeated request was to skinny spicy hushpuppies. The base ingredient is usually carb-rich cornmeal. My version adds fiber by replacing ½ of the cornmeal with crushed Fiber One Cereal, without losing flavor. I also use a low-fat buttermilk to cut down on fat and fat calories. Finally, I bake these as mini-muffins instead of deep-frying them. As a result, these spicy hushpuppies are a lower-carb version of a Louisiana staple!

Nonstick cooking spray
1 cup cornmeal
1 cup crushed Fiber One Cereal (Original)
2 tsp. sugar
1¼ tsp. baking powder
1½ tsp. salt

1 egg
1 cup low-fat buttermilk
1 tbsp. canola oil
1 jalapeño pepper, seeded and minced
½ onion, minced
⅛ tsp. Tabasco sauce

Preheat oven to 350 degrees. Spray a mini-muffin pan with nonstick cooking spray.

In a large bowl, combine cornmeal, crushed Fiber One, sugar, baking powder, and salt.

In a smaller bowl, combine egg, low-fat buttermilk, canola oil, jalapeño pepper, onion, and Tabasco sauce. Pour egg mixture into cornmeal mixture. Combine.

Scoop by tablespoonfuls into mini-muffin pan. Bake for 25-30 minutes. Remove from oven. Cool and serve.

Yield: 36 mini-muffins

Serving Size: 2 muffins

Nutrition Facts per Serving
Calories: 50, Fat calories: 10, Total fat: 2 g, Saturated fat: 0 g, Cholesterol: 10 mg, Sodium: 240 mg, Total carbohydrates: 10 g, Dietary fiber: 2 g, Sugar: less than 1 g, Protein 1 g

SOUPS

Skinny Crockpot Cajun Bean Soup

While many folks only take the slow cooker out during the fall and winter months, I prefer to keep mine on my countertop for year-round access. Beans are an amazing source of fiber, and I continued to skinny this dish by tossing the high-salt "seasoning packet" included in a 15-bean soup mix and replacing it with light Cajun seasoning. I also use low-sodium turkey sausage, reduced-sodium beef broth, and water. Finally, I can't call this a Louisiana dish without the trinity: chopped celery, green bell pepper, and onion. The result is an amazing weeknight meal waiting for you, loaded with fiber and protein.

1 bag 15-bean soup mix
3 stalks celery, chopped
1 onion, sliced
1 green bell pepper, chopped

½ lb. low-sodium turkey sausage, sliced
2 cans reduced-sodium beef broth
4 cups water
1 tbsp. light Cajun seasoning

Combine all ingredients in a slow cooker. Cover and cook on high for 7 hours. Serve.

Yield: 8-10 servings

Serving Size: 1 cup

Nutrition Facts per Serving
Calories: 220, Fat calories: 30, Total fat: 3.5 g, Saturated fat: 1 g, Cholesterol: 20 mg, Sodium: 400 mg, Total carbohydrates: 31 g, Dietary fiber: 7 g, Sugar: 2 g, Protein: 18 g

Traditional Bean Soup Nutrition Facts per Serving
Calories: 360, Total fat: 11 g, Sodium: 490 mg, Total carbohydrates: 53 g

Rockin' Crockpot Red Bean and Turkey Chili

Showcasing our main Louisiana bean as well as the sweet potato, our state vegetable, this crockpot chili makes a great weeknight meal. The beans provide fiber and the sweet potatoes add vitamin A. I continued to skinny the recipe by using lean ground turkey and light Cajun seasoning. Your family will be thrilled with this easy dish.

1 lb. 93 percent lean ground turkey
1 pkg. (1 lb.) frozen onion and green bell pepper mix
2 cans red beans, rinsed

1 can diced tomatoes
1 cup salsa
2 sweet potatoes, peeled and chopped
1 tbsp. light Cajun seasoning

Combine all ingredients in a slow cooker. Cover and cook on low for 6 hours or high for 4 hours. Serve.

Yield: 8-10 servings

Serving Size: 1 cup

Nutrition Facts per Serving
Calories: 266, Total fat: 8 g, Saturated fat: 1 g, Cholesterol: 35 mg, Sodium: 430 mg, Total carbohydrates: 22 g, Dietary fiber: 6 g, Sugar: 7 g, Protein: 14 g

Traditional Chili Nutrition Facts per Serving
Calories: 287, Total fat: 14.1 g, Sodium: 1,336 mg, Total carbohydrates: 30.5 g

Saint-Sational Crawfish and Sausage Chowder

Nothing makes me feel better on a cold, rainy day than flannel pajamas and a bowl of delicious chowder! Unfortunately, while warm and tasty, traditional crawfish or other seafood-based chowders can expand our waistlines due to the carbohydrates and fats in the flour, potatoes, corn, and heavy cream. I made simple, skinny changes to my chowder by decreasing the flour, eliminating potatoes and corn, and replacing heavy cream with a lower-fat half-and-half. The result is a delicious, skinny-ed chowder that will keep you warm during the cold, rainy season!

2 tbsp. olive oil
½ lb. low-sodium turkey sausage, sliced
1 onion, minced
2 stalks celery, minced
1 green bell pepper, minced
1 tbsp. minced garlic

2 tbsp. all-purpose flour
3 cans reduced-sodium chicken broth
2 tsp. light Cajun seasoning
¼ tsp. cayenne pepper
1 lb. crawfish tails, peeled and deveined
½ cup half-and-half

In a large stockpot or Dutch oven, heat olive oil over medium heat. Add sausage. Cook, stirring, for 5 minutes.

Add onions and celery. Cook for 5 minutes.

Add green pepper. Cook for 5-10 minutes or until soft.

Add garlic and cook for 1 minute.

Sprinkle flour over vegetables. Stirring constantly, cook for 2 minutes. Add chicken broth and stir.

Add light Cajun seasoning and cayenne pepper. Bring to a boil. Reduce to a simmer. Cook for 20 minutes.

Add crawfish and half-and-half. Cook for 5-10 minutes or until crawfish are heated through. Dish into soup bowls and serve.

Yield: About 10 servings

Serving Size: 1 cup

Nutrition Facts per Serving

Calories: 150, Fat calories: 70, Total fat: 8 g, Saturated fat: 2 g, Cholesterol: 75 mg, Sodium: 370 mg, Total carbohydrates: 5 g, Dietary fiber: less than 1 g, Sugar: 2 g, Protein: 16 g

Traditional Crawfish Chowder Nutrition Facts per Serving

Calories: 296, Total fat: 20.6 g, Sodium: 700 mg, Total carbohydrates: 15.4 g, Sugar: 4.5 g

Celebration Crawfish Soup

Soup is the best comfort food on a chilly day, and my Celebration Crawfish Soup is no exception to this rule. Don't get me wrong—I love a bisque or chowder, but sometimes the simplicity of a brothy soup just hits the spot. Most soups can be a part of a healthy diet, but we do have to watch for added sodium, calories, carbs, and fat. How did I make this soup fit into a healthy lifestyle? It was easy! By using a reduced-sodium broth and olive oil instead of butter, I decreased the sodium, calories, and fat. I punched up the nutrients and fiber by adding more vegetables, particularly celery and tomatoes. Finally, our Louisiana crawfish offers us a wonderful source of protein. The result is a great soup loaded with protein without all the sodium and fat.

1 tbsp. olive oil	1 lb. crawfish tails, peeled and deveined
1 onion, chopped	½ cup lemon juice
3 stalks celery, chopped	2 tbsp. chopped basil
1 green bell pepper, chopped	1 tsp. Tabasco pepper sauce
1 garlic clove, chopped	2 tsp. Worcestershire sauce
4 tomatoes, chopped	Dash of salt
3 cans reduced-sodium chicken broth	¼ cup half-and-half
2 cups water	

In a large stockpot or Dutch oven, heat olive oil over medium heat. Add onion. Cook for 3-5 minutes.

Add celery and bell pepper. Cook for 5-7 minutes. Add garlic and cook for 1 minute.

Add tomatoes, chicken broth, water, and crawfish. Bring to a boil.

Add lemon juice, basil, Tabasco, Worcestershire sauce, and salt. Reduce heat to low, and cook for 25-30 minutes.

Stir in half-and-half and serve.

Yield: **8-10 servings**

Serving Size: **1 cup**

Nutrition Facts per Serving
Calories: 90, Fat calories: 25, Total fat: 3 g, Saturated fat: 0.5 g, Cholesterol: 50 mg, Sodium: 90 mg, Total carbohydrates: 7 g, Dietary fiber: 1 g, Sugar: 3 g, Protein: 10 g

SuperFast Shrimp Chowder

Need a quick weeknight recipe on a chilly day? My Superfast Shrimp Chowder is not only pantry-friendly—it can be prepared in only 30 minutes. This soup is dependent on a well-stocked pantry, and many are concerned about purchasing canned items due to their high-sodium content. The great news? Reduced-sodium and reduced-fat broths and cream soups are readily available at local supermarkets, and these can be substituted into my recipes. I continued to skinny this dish by using 2 percent milk in place of whole milk. The shrimp adds an amazing amount of protein without tons of fat and calories. The result is a speedy, delicious soup that is lower in calories, sodium, and fat.

1 tbsp. canola oil

1 onion, chopped

1 can 98 percent fat-free or Healthy Request cream of mushroom soup

1 can 98 percent fat-free or Healthy Request cream of chicken soup

2 cups water

3 cups 2 percent milk

1 lb. fresh medium-size shrimp, peeled and deveined

1½ cups shredded part-skim mozzarella cheese

In a large stockpot or Dutch oven, heat oil over medium heat. Add onion. Cook for 5 minutes or until tender.

Add soups, water, and milk. Bring to a boil over medium-high heat.

Add shrimp and reduce heat. Simmer for 5-7 minutes or until shrimp turn pink.

Stir in cheese until melted. Serve.

Yield: *8-10 servings*

Serving Size: *1 cup*

Nutrition Facts per Serving
Calories: 150, Fat calories: 60, Total fat: 7 g, Saturated fat: 2.5 g, Cholesterol: 70 mg, Sodium: 570 mg, Total carbohydrates: 10 g, Dietary fiber: less than 1 g, Sugar: 5 g, Protein: 13 g

Traditional Shrimp Chowder Nutrition Facts per Serving
Calories: 260, Total fat: 17 g, Sodium: 640 mg, Total carbohydrates: 22 g, Sugar: 7 g

Vegetables

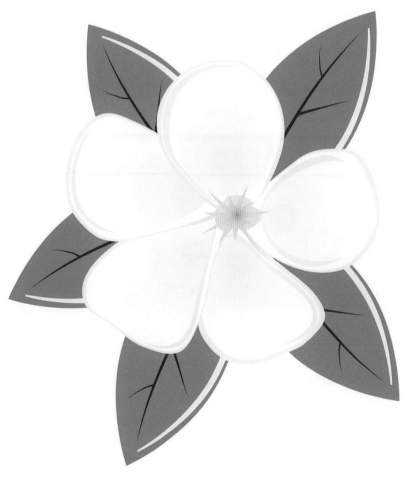

CaJUN ParMeSaN CauLiFLoWer BiteS

These baked, high-fiber cauliflower bites are kid-friendly and perfect for your next meal. I must admit, I have a weakness for fried items, but they are not the best for hips. These delicious baked bits are incredibly crunchy (not mushy) and have a secret ingredient—crushed Fiber One Cereal. Of course, I never share a recipe without my husband and kids approving. Guess what? They loved it!

¾ cup panko breadcrumbs, crushed
¾ cup Fiber One Cereal, crushed
½ cup grated Parmesan cheese

1 tsp. light Cajun seasoning
½ head cauliflower, cut into bite-size florets
2 eggs, whisked

Preheat oven to 400 degrees. Line a baking sheet with parchment paper or nonstick aluminum foil.

In a bowl, combine panko breadcrumbs, Fiber One, Parmesan cheese, and Cajun seasoning.

Dip cauliflower pieces into whisked eggs, roll in crumb mixture, and place on lined baking sheet. Continue until all cauliflower is coated. Bake for 25-30 minutes or until crunchy. Serve.

Yield: 4 servings

Nutrition Facts per Serving
Calories: 110, Fat calories: 70, Total fat: 8 g, Saturated fat: 1 g, Cholesterol: 0 mg, Sodium: 75 mg, Total carbohydrates: 10 g, Dietary fiber: 3 g, Sugar: 6 g, Protein: 2 g

Ravishing Roasted Okra

Many of us steer clear of this low-calorie powerhouse vegetable for one simple reason: it's slimy. But this dish isn't. I also eliminate the salt and let the okra's own amazing flavor shine. Another reason to eat up okra is that it can help reduce blood glucose levels in the diabetic population. A 2011 study in the Journal of Pharmacy & BioAllied Sciences linked the consumption of dried okra seeds to lower blood glucose levels.

1 pkg. frozen whole okra, thawed
1 tsp. olive oil
1 tsp. light Cajun seasoning

Preheat oven to 425 degrees. Line a baking sheet with parchment paper or aluminum foil. In a medium bowl, toss okra with olive oil and Cajun seasoning. Pour okra mixture onto the baking sheet. Arrange in 1 layer.

Bake for 15 minutes. Serve.

Yield: 4 servings

Nutrition Facts per Serving
Calories: 30, Fat calories: 10, Total fat: 1.5 g, Saturated fat: 0 g, Cholesterol: 0 mg, Sodium: 170 mg, Total carbohydrates: 5 g, Dietary fiber: 2 g, Sugar: 2 g, Protein: 1 g

Traditional Fried Okra Nutrition Facts per Serving
Calories: 266, Total fat: 8 g, Sodium: 32 mg, Total carbohydrates: 28 g

Outstanding Okra and Tomatoes

Many of us are familiar with the traditional Southern side dish of okra and tomatoes. It contains two powerhouse vegetables, but their benefits are often outweighed by lots of bacon, salt, and grease. No worries! A few simple skinny tricks transform this recipe into a Louisiana superfood dish. By using only 2 slices of turkey bacon, I decreased the fat, calories, and sodium. I further reduced the sodium by replacing the salt with light Cajun seasoning and using low-sodium canned diced tomatoes. The result is a flavorful, nutritious side dish without all the fat, calories, and sodium.

2 slices turkey bacon
Nonstick cooking spray
1 pkg. frozen sliced okra, thawed
1 onion, chopped
1 green bell pepper, chopped

3 stalks celery, chopped
1 can low-sodium diced tomatoes, undrained
1 tsp. light Cajun seasoning

Heat a medium skillet over medium heat. Cook bacon until brown. Crumble and set aside.

Spray skillet with nonstick cooking spray. Return to medium heat. Sauté okra, onion, pepper, and celery for 7-10 minutes.

Add tomatoes and Cajun seasoning. Cook for 5 minutes.

Remove from heat. Stir in crumbled bacon. Serve.

Yield: 4-6 servings

Serving Size: 1 cup

Nutrition Facts per Serving
Calories: 80, Fat calories: 15, Total fat: 1.5 g, Saturated fat: 0 g, Cholesterol: 5 mg, Sodium: 270 mg, Total carbohydrates: 14 g, Dietary fiber: 4 g, Sugar: 7 g, Protein: 4 g

Creole Tomato Salad

Many restaurants in the New Orleans area feature the Creole tomato in their salads and soups. This simple dish includes goat cheese, which is lower in sodium than other cheeses. This 5-ingredient, low-carb, tasty salad featuring Creole tomatoes will turn heads at your next romantic dinner or girls' night in. Do note that Creole tomatoes are not available year round, so Roma tomatoes may be substituted. But when Creole tomatoes are in the store, I always buy those!

2 Creole or 4 Roma tomatoes, sliced

4 oz. goat cheese, crumbled

1 tbsp. olive oil

¼ cup fresh basil, chopped

Cracked pepper

Lay sliced tomatoes on a plate or tray. Sprinkle goat cheese on tomatoes. Drizzle with olive oil and top with basil and cracked pepper. Serve.

Yield: 4-6 servings

Nutrition Facts per Serving

Calories: 80, Fat calories: 60, Total fat: 6 g, Saturated fat: 3 g, Cholesterol: 10 mg, Sodium: 90 mg, Total carbohydrates: 2 g, Dietary fiber: less than 1 g, Sugar: 2 g, Protein: 4 g

Tasty Tomato and Onion Salad

Change up your routine with this simple tomato and onion salad. Instead of drowning it with a creamy dressing, I toss the fresh vegetables with olive oil. One cup of this simple, low-calorie salad contains ¼ of our daily requirement of vitamin C.

4 medium tomatoes, cut into ½-inch chunks
½ onion, diced

2 tbsp. olive oil
1 tsp. light Cajun seasoning

In a medium bowl, toss tomatoes and onion together. Add olive oil and Cajun seasoning. Toss again and serve.

Yield: 4-6 servings

Serving Size: 1 cup

Nutrition Facts per Serving
Calories: 60, Fat calories: 40, Total fat: 4.5 g, Saturated fat: 0.5 g, Cholesterol: 0 mg, Sodium: 120 mg, Total carbohydrates: 4 g, Dietary fiber: 1 g, Sugar: 3 g, Protein: 1 g

CajuN TWo-Step RoaSted BroccoLi

Broccoli—you love it or you hate it. Plain broccoli may not be the most appetizing side dish, but drowning these "baby trees" in butter and salt spells trouble for your heart and waistline. Instead, skinny up broccoli by using olive oil and light Cajun seasoning and then roasting the florets in the oven. I promise that this dish will become a staple in your home.

1 bunch broccoli, cut into florets
2 tsp. olive oil

1 garlic clove, chopped
½ tsp. light Cajun seasoning

Preheat oven to 400 degrees. Line a baking sheet with parchment paper or aluminum foil.

In a medium bowl, toss broccoli with olive oil, garlic, and Cajun seasoning. Pour broccoli mixture onto the baking sheet. Arrange in 1 layer.

Bake for 15-20 minutes. Serve.

Yield: 4 servings

Serving Size: 1 cup

Nutrition Facts per Serving
Calories: 70, Fat calories: 25, Total fat: 3 g, Saturated fat: 0 g, Cholesterol: 0 mg, Sodium: 135 mg, Total carbohydrates: 10 mg, Dietary fiber: 4 g, Sugar: 3 g, Protein: 4 g

Brilliantly Roasted Brussels Sprouts

While Brussels sprouts often get the "ew" response in my office, I promise that you will fall in love with the roasted version of this vegetable. Similar to my other roasted vegetable dishes, I eliminated the salt and used light Cajun seasoning for an amazing favor. It's a good thing that these yummy vegetables are low in calories, because I guarantee you will go for seconds.

1 pkg. (1 lb.) whole Brussels sprouts
1 tsp. canola oil
1 tsp. light Cajun seasoning

Preheat oven to 400 degrees. Line a baking sheet with parchment paper or aluminum foil.

With a sharp knife, cut Brussels sprouts in half lengthwise. In a medium bowl, toss Brussels sprouts with canola oil, and Cajun seasoning. Pour Brussels sprouts mixture onto the baking sheet. Arrange in 1 layer.

Bake for 20-25 minutes. Serve.

Yield: **4 servings**

Nutrition Facts per Serving
Calories: 60, Fat calories: 15, Total fat: 1.5 g, Saturated fat: 0 g, Cholesterol: 0 mg, Sodium: 200 mg, Total carbohydrates: 10 g, Dietary fiber: 4 g, Sugar: 2 g, Protein: 4 g

RagiN' CajUN RoaSted ArticHoKeS

Artichoke is the first vegetable that I insist my clients prepare. The reason? Artichokes are one of the highest-fiber vegetables, with 1 serving providing over 30 percent of our daily fiber requirements. And don't worry—I used frozen artichoke hearts in this recipe to speed up preparation time. You will love this dish!

1 pkg. frozen artichoke hearts, thawed
1 tsp. olive oil
½ tsp. light Cajun seasoning

Preheat oven to 400 degrees. Line a baking sheet with parchment paper or aluminum foil.

In a medium bowl, toss artichokes with olive oil and Cajun seasoning. Pour artichoke mixture onto the baking sheet. Arrange in 1 layer.

Bake for 40-50 minutes. Serve.

Yield: 4 servings

Nutrition Facts per Serving
Calories: 60, Fat calories: 10, Total fat: 1 g, Saturated fat: 0 g, Cholesterol: 0 mg, Sodium: 150 mg, Total carbohydrates: 8 g, Dietary fiber: 5 g, Sugar: 3 g, Protein: 3 g

Spicy Sautéed Mushrooms

I am addicted to mushrooms. Many of my clients give me an eyebrow raise, but a serving of mushrooms is quite low in calories and packs a huge nutritional punch with niacin, selenium, and riboflavin. This flavorful side dish is ready in about 15 minutes, and it will quickly become a family favorite.

1 tsp. canola oil
1 pkg. (10-12 oz.) whole white mushrooms, washed and dried

1 tsp. reduced-sodium soy sauce
1 tsp. light Cajun seasoning

In a medium saucepan, heat canola oil over medium heat. Add mushrooms. Sauté for 7-10 minutes.

Add soy sauce and Cajun seasoning. Stir. Cook for 5 minutes.

Remove from heat and serve.

Yield: *4 servings*

Nutrition Facts per Serving
Calories: 25, Fat calories: 10, Total fat: 1 g, Saturated fat: 0 g, Cholesterol: 0 mg, Sodium: 210 mg, Total carbohydrates: 3 g, Dietary fiber: 0 g, Sugar: 1 g, Protein: 2 g

So-Sweet Satsuma-Glazed Sweet Potatoes

Our glorious state vegetable, the sweet potato, is a Louisiana superfood. Unfortunately, we usually turn this amazing source of vitamin A into a super dud by preparing traditional casseroles with lots of butter and brown sugar. While such a dish is common at Thanksgiving and Christmas, you will love my surprisingly sweet skinny twist using satsumas and just 1 tbsp. brown sugar. Trust me, your family will be begging for this Louisiana superfood dish.

2 medium-size sweet potatoes
1 tbsp. vanilla extract
1 tbsp. brown sugar
½ tsp. satsuma or orange zest

¼ cup satsuma juice (or 100 percent orange juice)
1 tsp. olive oil
¼ tsp. cinnamon

Preheat oven to 325 degrees. Line a 9x13 baking pan with parchment paper or aluminum foil.

Peel potatoes. Cut into 1-inch-thick slices. In a medium bowl, toss sweet-potato slices with vanilla, brown sugar, satsuma or orange zest, satsuma or orange juice, olive oil, and cinnamon.

Pour sweet-potato mixture into the baking pan. Cover with foil. Bake for 45-50 minutes. Uncover and bake for 5-10 minutes.

Remove from oven. Serve.

Yield: **4 servings**

Nutrition Facts per Serving
Calories: 100, Fat calories: 10, Total fat: 1 g, Saturated fat: 0 g, Cholesterol: 0 mg, Sodium: 35 mg, Total carbohydrates: 10 g, Dietary fiber: 2 g, Sugar: 8 g, Protein: 1 g

Traditional Sweet-Potato Casserole Nutrition Facts per Serving
Calories: 270, Total fat: 6 g, Sodium: 110 mg, Total carbohydrates: 54 g, Sugar: 42 g

Sizzling Sweet-potato Fries

What's not to love about the sweet potato? Not only is it the Louisiana state vegetable, but it is low in calories. I gave this dish a skinny twist by baking instead of frying the sweet potatoes. Trust me, the time it takes to prepare this recipe is worth it!

2 sweet potatoes, peeled and cut into strips
1 tbsp. canola oil
1 tsp. light Cajun seasoning

Preheat oven to 400 degrees. Line a baking sheet with parchment paper or aluminum foil.

In a medium bowl, toss sweet-potato strips with canola oil and Cajun seasoning. Pour sweet-potato mixture onto the baking sheet. Arrange in 1 layer.

Bake for 40 minutes. Remove from oven. Toss.

Turn oven to broil. Return sweet potatoes to oven. Cook for 3-5 minutes.

Remove from broiler. Serve.

Yield: *4 servings*

Nutrition Facts per Serving
Calories: 90, Fat calories: 30, Total fat: 3.5 g, Saturated fat: 0 g, Cholesterol: 0 mg, Sodium: 210 mg, Total carbohydrates: 13 g, Dietary fiber: 2 g, Sugar: 3 g, Protein: 1 g

Traditional Sweet-Potato Fries Nutrition Facts per Serving
Calories: 295, Total fat: 14 g, Sodium: 114 mg, Total carbohydrates: 22 g, Sugar: 9 g

King Cake Sweet-potato Fries

While many restaurants coat their sweet-potato fries with sugar and serve them with a ton of sweet dipping sauce, I drizzled—not drowned—this dish with Mardi Gras sugar. Celebrate our state vegetable the skinny way!

1 sweet potato, peeled and sliced into thin strips
Nonstick cooking spray

1 tsp. 2 percent milk
⅛ tsp. almond extract
¼ tsp. each purple, green, and gold sugar

Preheat oven to 400 degrees. Line a baking sheet with parchment paper or aluminum foil.

Line up potato strips on baking sheet. Spray with nonstick cooking spray. Bake for 20 minutes.

Remove from oven. Toss. Return to oven and bake for 10 minutes.

Increase heat to broil. Cook for 2-3 minutes.

Remove from oven. Place on serving plate and allow to cool slightly.

In a small bowl, combine milk and almond extract. Drizzle mixture over cooled potatoes. Sprinkle sugar over potatoes. Serve.

Yield: **2 servings**

Nutrition Facts per Serving
Calories: 70 calories, Fat calories: 0, Total fat: 0 g, Saturated fat: 0 g, Cholesterol: 0 mg, Sodium: 35 mg, Total carbohydrates: 15 g, Dietary fiber: 2 g, Sugar: 5 g, Protein: 1 g

Traditional Sweet-Potato Fries Nutrition Facts per Serving
Calories: 295, Total fat: 14 g, Sodium: 114 g, Total carbohydrates: 22 g, Sugar: 9 g

Mardi Gras Slaw

Feel great serving this dish, since it not only reflects the gorgeous hues of Mardi Gras but also offers an amazing source of vitamins A and C and omega-3. How did I skinny this slaw? While many versions contain up to ¹/₂ cup sugar, I reduced the amount to 1 tbsp. To add a bit of flair from our fabulous state, I included cayenne pepper and light Cajun seasoning and then topped the dish with pecans.

½ head red cabbage, shredded
½ head green cabbage, shredded
2 yellow bell peppers, thinly sliced
2 green bell peppers, thinly sliced
1 tsp. cumin
1 tsp. light Cajun seasoning

1 tsp. cayenne pepper
1 tbsp. sugar*
⅓ cup lemon juice
⅓ cup olive oil
⅓ cup chopped pecans*

In a large bowl, toss cabbage and bell peppers together.

In a small bowl, combine cumin, Cajun seasoning, cayenne pepper, sugar, lemon juice, and olive oil. Pour over cabbage mixture. Toss. Sprinkle with pecans and serve.

*Feel free to use your favorite sugar substitute and nuts to make this recipe your own.

Yield: 12 servings

Serving Size: 1 cup

Nutrition Facts per Serving
Calories: 110, Fat calories: 70, Total fat: 8 g, Saturated fat: 1 g, Cholesterol: 0 mg, Sodium: 75 mg, Total carbohydrates: 10 g, Dietary fiber: 3 g, Sugar: 6 g, Protein: 2 g

Traditional Cole Slaw Nutrition Facts per Serving
Calories: 236, Total fat: 18 g, Sodium: 665 mg, Total carbohydrates: 20 g, Sugar: 14 g

Cajun Edamame

While many of us know this high-protein, high-fiber soybean only as a dish served at our favorite Asian restaurants, we can find steam-in-the-bag edamame beans in the freezer sections of our local supermarkets. One serving of this two-ingredient recipe provides over 25 percent of our daily fiber requirements.

1 pkg. steam-in-the-bag shelled edamame
   beans
1 tsp. light Cajun seasoning

Prepare the edamame according to pkg. directions. While still warm, toss edamame with Cajun seasoning. Serve.

Yield: 4 servings

Nutrition Facts per Serving
Calories: 125, Fat calories: 45, Total fat: 5 g, Saturated fat: 0 g, Cholesterol: 0 mg, Sodium: 180 mg, Total carbohydrates: 9 g, Dietary fiber: 5 g, Sugar: 3 g, Protein: 11 g

CASSEROLES AND DRESSINGS

Skinny Cajun Shrimp Casserole

Casseroles are a Louisiana staple, yet so many of my diabetic clients feel they can never have them again because of the rice. Guess what? You can! I skinny-ed this dish by switching to a lower-fat cream soup mixed with our low-calorie, protein-rich shrimp as the meat. Then I replaced half the rice with the vegetable superstar, cauliflower. I promise that the taste is the same!

1 pkg. frozen steam-in-the-bag cauliflower
1 tbsp. canola oil
1 red onion, chopped
1 pkg. frozen onion and green bell pepper mix, thawed
2 garlic cloves, minced
2 cups frozen sliced okra
1 tbsp. lemon juice
2 tsp. light Cajun seasoning

1 pkg. (10-16 oz.) frozen shrimp, peeled and deveined, thawed
1 can (10¾ oz.) of 98 percent fat-free or Healthy Request cream of mushroom soup
½ cup water
1 tbsp. light soy sauce
½ tsp. cayenne pepper
1 cup cooked brown rice

Preheat oven to 350 degrees. Line a 9x13 baking pan with parchment paper or aluminum foil.

Microwave cauliflower for 1 minute less than recommended pkg. directions. Remove from microwave and chop cauliflower. Set aside.

In a large pan over medium-high heat, heat canola oil. Add cooked cauliflower, red onion, and onion and pepper mix. Cook for 7-9 minutes.

Add garlic. Sauté for 1 minute. Stir in okra, lemon juice, and Cajun seasoning.

Add shrimp. Cook for 5-7 minutes or until shrimp turn pink.

Stir in soup, water, soy sauce, cayenne pepper, and cooked rice. Pour mixture into prepared baking pan. Bake for 15-20 minutes.

Yield: 8-10 servings

Nutrition Facts per Serving
Calories: 170, Fat calories: 35, Total fat: 4 g, Saturated fat: 0 g, Cholesterol: 85 mg, Sodium: 450 mg, Total carbohydrates: 19 g, Dietary fiber: 3 g, Sugar: 5 g, Protein: 15 g

Mardi Gras Mambo Cajun Rice Dressing

I grew up with rice dressing, and one of my goals was to skinny this popular dish. I kissed the extra carbs goodbye by replacing some of the rice with cauliflower, and I used ground sirloin to decrease fat and calories. The result? You will be dancing the Mardi Gras mambo for this dressing!

Nonstick cooking spray
1 pkg. frozen steam-in-the-bag cauliflower
1 lb. 90 percent lean ground sirloin
1 tsp. canola oil
1 onion, chopped
3 stalks celery, chopped

1 green bell pepper, chopped
1 cup brown rice, uncooked
1 tsp. light Cajun seasoning
2 drops hot sauce (I used Tabasco)
1 can reduced-sodium chicken broth

Preheat oven to 350 degrees. Spray a 9x13 baking pan with nonstick cooking spray.

Microwave cauliflower for 1 minute less than recommended pkg. directions. Remove from microwave and chop cauliflower. Set aside.

In a large pan over medium-high heat, cook sirloin until no longer pink. Remove from pan.

Add oil to pan. Return to medium-high heat. Add onion, celery, and green pepper. Sauté for 5-7 minutes. Remove from heat.

Add cooked cauliflower, cooked sirloin, rice, Cajun seasoning, hot sauce, and chicken broth. Mix well. Pour mixture into baking pan. Cover with foil and bake for 60-70 minutes.

Yield: 8-10 servings

Nutrition Facts per Serving
Calories: 240, Fat calories: 70, Total fat: 8 g, Saturated fat: 1.5 g, Cholesterol: 40 mg, Sodium: 240 mg, Total carbohydrates: 22 g, Dietary fiber: 2 g, Sugar: 2 g, Protein: 19 g

Excellent Eggplant Rice Dressing

When I ask individuals if they enjoy eggplant, I often hear, "Eh." But this low-carb vegetable with only 20 calories per cup makes a great addition to traditional rice dressing, taking it from "eh" to excellent. This dish will not disappoint!

1 pkg. frozen steam-in-the-bag cauliflower
1 tsp. canola oil
1 lb. 93 percent lean ground turkey
1 large eggplant, peeled and chopped
1 onion, chopped
3 stalks celery, chopped

1 green bell pepper, chopped
½ cup chopped green onions
1 can reduced-sodium chicken broth
1 tsp. light Cajun seasoning
¾ cup cooked brown rice

Microwave cauliflower for 1 minute less than recommended pkg. directions. Remove from microwave and chop cauliflower. Set aside.

In a large skillet that has a lid, cook oil and ground turkey over medium heat, uncovered, for 5-7 minutes or until meat is no longer pink. Reduce heat.

Add cauliflower, eggplant, onion, celery, green pepper, and green onions. Cover and simmer for 15 minutes.

Add broth. Stir in seasoning, increase heat, and bring to a boil. Reduce heat and simmer, uncovered, for 30 minutes.

Stir in cooked rice until well mixed. Serve.

Yield: 8-10 servings

Nutrition Facts per Serving
Calories: 170, Fat calories: 70, Total fat: 7 g, Saturated fat: 1.5 g, Cholesterol: 40 mg, Sodium: 170 mg, Total carbohydrates: 13 g, Dietary fiber: 4 g, Sugar: 4 g, Protein: 14 g

SHeLLy'S SKiNNy GRits

I absolutely love grits. While I can't pinpoint the first time I tasted them, I can guarantee it was when I was wearing a diaper. Unfortunately, grits dishes can have a ton of fat and carbs. Here I switched from a stick of butter to 1 tbsp. canola oil. And replacing some of the grits with cauliflower reduces the carbs. This dish will be your new Saturday-morning staple.

1 pkg. frozen steam-in-the-bag cauliflower
3 cups water
¾ cup quick-cooking grits
2 cups 2 percent milk

1 cup half-and-half
1 tbsp. canola oil
Shredded 2 percent cheddar cheese

Microwave cauliflower for 1 minute less than pkg. directions. Remove from microwave and chop cauliflower. Set aside.

In a medium saucepan, boil water. Add grits and stir. When grits thicken, add milk, half-and-half, chopped cauliflower, and canola oil. Return to a boil.

Reduce heat to a simmer and cook for 45 minutes to 1 hour. Ladle cauliflower grits into bowls and garnish with cheese.

Yield: 6-8 servings

Nutrition Facts per Serving
Calories: 100, Fat calories: 60, Total fat: 7 g, Saturated fat: 3 g, Cholesterol: 15 mg, Sodium: 80 mg, Total carbohydrates: 8 g, Dietary fiber: 1 g, Sugar: 5 g, Protein: 4 g

Second Helping Grits and Sausage Casserole

"I don't like grits." These words from my Yankee husband made me cry. After wiping away my tears, I took the challenge to make grits both skinny and husband-approved. I replaced some of the grits with our superstar cauliflower, switched to a 2 percent milk and cheddar cheese, added sliced chicken sausage, and crossed my fingers. I knew I'd succeeded when my husband went back for a second helping.

Nonstick cooking spray
1 pkg. frozen steam-in-the-bag cauliflower
1 lb. chicken sausage, sliced
2 cups water
½ cup quick-cooking grits

4 eggs
1½ cups shredded 2 percent cheddar cheese
½ cup 2 percent milk
1 tbsp. canola oil

Preheat oven to 350 degrees. Spray a 9x13 baking pan with nonstick cooking spray.

Microwave cauliflower for 1 minute less than recommended pkg. directions. Remove from microwave and chop cauliflower. Set aside.

In a large skillet over medium heat, cook chicken sausage for 7-10 minutes or until no longer pink. Drain and set aside.

In a saucepan over medium heat, boil water. Stir in grits. Add chopped cauliflower. Reduce heat and cook for 4-5 minutes. Remove from heat.

Stir eggs into grits. Mix well. Add sausage, 1 cup cheese, milk, and oil. Mix well.

Pour mixture into prepared baking pan. Sprinkle with remaining cheese. Bake for 50-60 minutes.

Yield: 10 servings

Nutrition Facts per Serving
Calories: 210, Fat calories: 120, Total fat: 14 g, Saturated fat: 5 g, Cholesterol: 155 mg, Sodium: 640 mg, Total carbohydrates: 5 g, Dietary fiber: less than 1 g, Sugar: 1 g, Protein: 16 g

Jump For Joy Jambalaya Grits

This dish combines two of my favorites—jambalaya and grits. The combination may seem a bit odd, but the grits play the role of the rice in the jambalaya, and the taste will make you jump for joy. As in my other one-pot meals, I skinny-ed this dish by using a lower-fat, lower-sodium chicken sausage, replaced half of the grits with cauliflower, and substituted 2 percent milk for whole milk.

1 pkg. frozen steam-in-the-bag cauliflower	¼ lb. chicken sausage, sliced
1 tbsp. canola oil	¼ lb. low-sodium ham, diced
1 onion, chopped	2 Roma tomatoes, chopped
1 green bell pepper, chopped	3 cups 2 percent milk
3 stalks celery, chopped	1 cup quick-cooking grits
¼ tsp. light Cajun seasoning	Nonstick cooking spray
¼ tsp. black pepper	½ lb. shrimp, peeled and deveined
¼ tsp. cayenne pepper	½ cup shredded 2 percent cheddar cheese

Microwave cauliflower for 1 minute less than recommended pkg. directions. Remove from microwave and chop cauliflower. Set aside.

In a large skillet over medium-high heat, add canola oil, cooked cauliflower, onion, green pepper, celery, Cajun seasoning, black pepper, and cayenne pepper. Sauté for 5-7 minutes or until vegetables are soft.

Add sausage and ham. Cook for 2 minutes.

Add tomatoes. Cook for 2 minutes.

Add milk. Bring to a boil. Reduce heat to medium.

Add grits. Cook and stir for 7-8 minutes.

While mixture is cooking, spay a medium skillet with nonstick cooking spray. Heat over medium heat and add shrimp. Cook for 5-7 minutes or until no longer pink.

Stir shrimp into grits. Stir in cheese until melted. Serve.

Yield: 10 servings

Nutrition Facts per Serving
Calories: 170, Fat calories: 70, Total fat: 7 g, Saturated fat: 3 g, Cholesterol: 65 mg, Sodium: 420 mg, Total carbohydrates: 11 g, Dietary fiber: 2 g, Sugar: 6 g, Protein: 16 g

Not Your Mama's Cabbage Jambalaya

Jambalaya is an amazing combination of flavors and spices that makes my heart sing and my hips scream. You will be surprised by the simple solutions I used to make this dish a Skinny Louisiana favorite. Lean ground turkey reduces fat, and a secret ingredient, cabbage, adds a ton of nutrients without all of the calories and carbs. You will love this!

1 pkg. frozen steam-in-the-bag cauliflower
1 lb. 93 percent lean ground turkey
1 onion, chopped
3 stalks celery, chopped
1 green bell pepper, chopped
1 garlic clove, chopped

1 medium head green cabbage, chopped
1 can (14.5 oz.) diced tomatoes, undrained
½ cup water
¼ cup brown rice, uncooked
1 tsp. light Cajun seasoning

Microwave cauliflower for 1 minute less than recommended pkg. directions. Remove from microwave and chop cauliflower. Set aside.

In a large pan over medium heat, cook ground turkey, onion, celery, green pepper, and garlic for 7-10 minutes or until turkey is brown.

Stir in cabbage, tomatoes, water, rice, cooked cauliflower, and Cajun seasoning. Bring to a boil.

Reduce heat to low. Cover and cook for 35-45 minutes.

Yield: 8-10 servings

Nutrition Facts per Serving
Calories: 160, Fat calories: 45, Total fat: 5 g, Saturated fat: 3 g, Cholesterol: 40 mg, Sodium: 170 mg, Total carbohydrates: 15 g, Dietary fiber: 5 g, Sugar: 6 g, Protein: 14 g

Walk on the Wild Side Squash Casserole

While many focus on steaming squash, take a walk on the wild side and prepare it in this casserole instead. While traditional casseroles use crumbled crackers as a topping, I gave this one a skinny twist by substituting crushed All-Bran Flakes, which decreases the carbs but maintains a great crunch. Go ahead, get wild!

Nonstick cooking spray
1 tbsp. canola oil
6 yellow squash, thinly sliced
1 onion, sliced
½ cup shredded reduced-fat Parmesan
   cheese

1 cup shredded 2 percent cheddar cheese
½ cup light sour cream
1 cup crushed All-Bran Flakes

Preheat oven to 350 degrees. Spray a 2-qt. casserole dish with nonstick cooking spray.

In a large skillet over medium heat, add oil, squash, and onion. Sauté until vegetables are soft.

Pour mixture into a large bowl. Add Parmesan, shredded cheddar, and sour cream. Toss.

Pour mixture into prepared casserole dish. Sprinkle crushed All-Bran evenly over top of mixture. Bake for 20-25 minutes or until top is golden and bubbly.

Yield: 8-10 servings

Nutrition Facts per Serving. Calories: 120, Fat calories: 60, Total fat: 7 g, Saturated fat: 3.5 g, Cholesterol: 15 mg, Sodium: 170 mg, Total carbohydrates: 9 g, Dietary fiber: 2 g, Sugar: 4 g, Protein: 6 g

Loaded Cauliflower Casserole

You say macaroni; I say cauliflower! That's right. I took the yummy flavors of a loaded macaroni-and-cheese casserole and transformed them into a lower-carb, diabetic-friendly, loaded cauliflower casserole. I promise this is a winner!

Nonstick cooking spray
2 pkg. frozen steam-in-the-bag cauliflower
1 cup shredded 2 percent cheddar cheese
1 cup shredded mozzarella cheese
8 oz. light cream cheese, softened

¼ cup fat-free half-and-half
½ chopped cup green onions
2 slices turkey bacon, cooked and crumbled
¼ tsp. light Cajun seasoning

Preheat oven to 350 degrees. Spray a 2-qt. casserole dish with nonstick cooking spray.

Microwave cauliflower for 1 minute less than recommended pkg. directions. Remove from microwave and chop cauliflower. Set aside.

In a medium bowl, combine cheddar, mozzarella, light cream cheese, and half-and-half. Stir in green onions, crumbled bacon, and Cajun seasoning. Add cauliflower to mixture.

Pour mixture into prepared casserole dish. Cover with foil. Bake for 25 minutes.

Remove foil. Bake for 5-10 more minutes or until bubbly.

Yield: 10 servings

Nutrition Facts per Serving
Calories: 180, Fat calories: 110, Total fat: 7 g, Cholesterol: 40 mg, Sodium: 350 mg, Total carbohydrates: 5 g, Dietary fiber: 1 g, Sugar: 2 g, Protein: 12 g

Traditional Macaroni-and-Cheese Casserole Nutrition Facts per Serving
Calories: 344, Total fat: 12 g, Sodium: 339 mg, Total carbohydrates: 24 g

Skinny Cajun Stuffed Bell Peppers

Growing up, I was addicted to stuffed bell peppers. The problem? My childhood version of this dish was loaded with breadcrumbs, butter, and higher-fat cuts of meat. In my simple skinny solution, I kissed the breadcrumbs goodbye, used a fat-free half-and-half, and switched over to a lean ground sirloin.

Nonstick cooking spray

Water

5 green or red bell peppers, halved lengthwise and cored

1 lb. 90 percent lean ground sirloin

1 onion, chopped

3 stalks celery, chopped

1 green bell pepper, chopped

½ tsp. light Cajun seasoning

½ tsp. black pepper

⅓ cup grated reduced-fat Parmesan cheese

¼ cup fat-free half-and-half

1 tbsp. Worcestershire sauce

Preheat oven to 350 degrees. Spray a 9x13 baking pan with nonstick cooking spray.

Over high heat, boil a large stockpot of water.

Add bell pepper halves to water. Cook for 5 minutes. Remove from pot.

In a large saucepan or skillet over medium-high heat, cook ground sirloin, onion, celery, and chopped bell pepper for 5-7 minutes or until sirloin no longer pink.

Stir in Cajun seasoning, black pepper, cheese, half-and-half, and Worcestershire sauce. Cook for 1 minute. Remove from heat.

Fill peppers with meat mixture and place in prepared baking pan. Bake for 15-20 minutes.

Yield: *5 servings*

Nutrition Facts per Serving
Calories: 230, Fat calories: 100, Total fat: 11 g, Saturated fat: 4.5, Cholesterol: 65 mg, Sodium: 290 mg, Total carbohydrates: 11 g, Dietary fiber: 3 g, Sugar: 6 g, Protein: 21 g

Baked Sweet-potato and Zucchini "Fritters"

Who doesn't love a fritter? The first bite brings fat, the second bite brings calories, and the third bite brings carbs. Instead of frying, I turned to the oven to skinny this dish, and I promise you will not be disappointed.

1 tbsp. canola oil
1 large egg
2 tsp. light Cajun seasoning
1 tsp. black pepper

2 tbsp. all-purpose flour
1 sweet potato, peeled and grated
2 large zucchini, peeled and grated

Preheat oven to 375 degrees. Line 2 baking sheets with parchment paper or aluminum foil.

In a medium bowl, combine canola oil and egg. Whisk. Stir in Cajun seasoning and pepper.

Add flour. Stir.

Add sweet potato and zucchini. Toss until all ingredients are combined.

Using a ½-cup measuring cup, scoop fritter mixture from bowl and form into fritters on baking sheets. Bake for 10 minutes.

Reduce heat to 350 degrees. Bake for 15 minutes. Remove from oven. Using a spatula, carefully flip fritters.

Return to oven and bake for an additional 15 minutes or until brown.

Remove from oven and allow to cool. Serve.

Yield: 4-6 servings

Serving Size: 1 fritter

Nutrition Facts per Serving
Calories: 70, Fat calories: 30, Total fat: 3 g, Saturated fat: 0 g, Cholesterol: 30 mg, Sodium: 310 mg, Total carbohydrates: less than 1 g, Dietary fiber: 1 g, Sugar: 1 g, Protein: 2 g

CHICKEN

Dazzling Chicken Salad Remoulade

New Orleans restaurants always offer a delicious remoulade dish on their lunch menus. From accompanying crab cakes to starring in a shrimp salad, remoulade spices up any meal. Unfortunately, it adds both fat and calories to the dish. I slimmed down this traditional mayonnaise-based sauce by using a combination of light mayonnaise and Greek yogurt. Greek yogurt makes an incredible substitution for mayonnaise in any dip or spread, since it adds a power punch of protein and calcium without all the fat and calories. Serve this yummy chicken salad over fresh greens or in a high-fiber wrap for lunch on a hot summer day.

1 tsp. lemon zest	¼ tsp. celery salt
½ cup light mayonnaise	½ tsp. Tabasco pepper sauce
¼ cup Greek yogurt	½ small red onion, chopped
1 tbsp. spicy mustard	½ bell pepper, chopped
1 tsp. paprika	1 stalk celery, chopped
1 tbsp. ketchup	1 lb. cooked chicken breast, chopped

In a bowl, combine lemon zest, light mayonnaise, Greek yogurt, spicy mustard, paprika, ketchup, celery salt, and Tabasco pepper sauce. Whisk until well blended.

Add red onion, bell pepper, and celery. Toss lightly. Add chicken, and toss again. Chill before serving.

Yield: 8 servings

Nutrition Facts per Serving
Calories: 210, Fat calories: 120, Total fat: 13 g, Saturated fat: 2.5 g, Cholesterol: 30 mg, Sodium: 440 mg, Total carbohydrates: 13 g, Dietary fiber: 1 g, Sugar: 2 g, Protein: 10 g

Crispy and Skinny Cajun Chicken Pizza

This amazing pizza has it all—taste, crispiness, and a bit of Cajun zing! While we may think we are eating a healthier lunch than the traditional drive-thru burger and fries by selecting pizza, the average 2 slices of pepperoni pizza have 580 calories, 24 grams of fat, and 65 grams of carbs. For a skinny alternative, replace the pepperoni with cooked chicken breast, a great source of protein without all the fat and calories in the pepperoni, and add lots of vegetables, which offer fiber, crunch, and flavor but few calories. The most impressive improvement here is the crust. By using a high-fiber wrap (my favorite is Flatout Flatbread), I not only saved time by not having to prepare a homemade crust, but I also hiked up the fiber without the added carbs and fat!

2 Flatout Flatbread wraps
Nonstick cooking spray
Dash of light Cajun seasoning
2 tbsp. pizza sauce
½ bell pepper, sliced

¼ red onion, sliced
¼ cup sliced mushrooms
3 oz. cooked chicken breast, sliced
¼ cup shredded mozzarella cheese

Preheat oven to 350 degrees. Line a baking sheet with parchment paper. Place wraps on parchment paper, and spray with nonstick cooking spray. Bake for 2 minutes. Remove.

In a small bowl, whisk light Cajun seasoning with pizza sauce. Spread sauce on wraps. Layer with pepper, onion, mushrooms, and chicken. Top with shredded mozzarella cheese.

Bake for 8-10 minutes. Cut each pizza into 8 slices. Serve.

Yield: 2 pizzas

Serving Size: 1 pizza or 8 slices

Nutrition Facts per Serving
Calories: 200, Fat calories: 100, Total fat: 11 g, Saturated Fat: 3.5 g, Cholesterol: 35 mg, Sodium: 610 mg, Total carbohydrates: 18 g, Dietary fiber: 11 g, Sugar: 2 g, Protein: 18 g

Traditional Pepperoni Pizza Nutrition Facts per Serving (2 Slices)
Calories: 580, Total fat: 24 g, Total carbohydrates: 65 g

Brilliant Blueberry Chicken Burgers

Are you a fan of the local farmers' market? Do you love to go blueberry picking? If so, I have the perfect savory recipe starring this delicious fruit. I know what you are thinking: my mama never made blueberry burgers! I understand, but chew on this thought. Blueberry farms are common in Louisiana, and according to the LSU AgCenter, rabbiteye blueberries can be successfully grown in most areas of our gorgeous state except the coast. Blueberries increase the juiciness of a chicken burger, while panko breadcrumbs and crushed Fiber One Cereal reduce the carbs that come from traditional breadcrumbs. Be sure to serve these burgers on whole-wheat slider buns to keep the carb count down.

1 lb. ground chicken
½ tsp. light Cajun seasoning
¼ tsp. cayenne pepper
2 tbsp. panko breadcrumbs

2 tbsp. crushed Fiber One Cereal
1 egg
1 cup blueberries
4 whole-wheat slider buns

In a large bowl, and using clean hands, combine ground chicken, Cajun seasoning, cayenne pepper, panko breadcrumbs, crushed Fiber One Cereal, and egg. Add blueberries.

Form into 4 patties. Place the patties on a clean plate and refrigerate for 10 minutes.

Place burgers on a grill and cook for approximately 7 minutes per side.

Remove from grill. Serve on whole-wheat slider buns.

Yield: 4 burgers

Nutrition Facts per Serving
Calories: 210, Fat calories: 100, Total fat: 11 g, Saturated fat: 3 g, Cholesterol: 145 mg, Sodium: 270 mg, Total carbohydrates: 9 g, Dietary fiber: 2 g, Sugar: 4 g, Protein: 22 g

Traditional Whopper Hamburger Nutrition Facts per Serving
Calories: 490, Total Fat: 22 g, Total carbohydrates: 48 g

Skinny Louisiana Cajun Chicken Pasta

I must be honest—I love any Louisiana pasta dish. The richness, the spiciness, the creaminess, and yes, the calories: a lunch portion (which is smaller than a dinner serving) of a Cajun pasta can pack approximately 1,400 calories, 60 grams of fat, and 120 grams of carbs! Where does one start to skinny this dish? First, I used a grilled chicken instead of a crispy, fried one to decrease the fat, calories, and even carbs (remember, fried chicken is coated in flour). I then drastically lowered the fat in the sauce by switching out the heavy cream for half-and-half and reduced-fat cream cheese and Parmesan cheese. Finally, the serving size for this dish is important—²/₃ cup high-fiber pasta, to control the carb count. Be sure to select a whole-grain pasta with 5 grams of fiber or higher. Serve this dish with a vegetable on the side, and you have an amazing meal that the entire family will love.

2 tsp. canola oil
2 green bell peppers, chopped
½ red onion, chopped
1 cup chopped mushrooms
½ tsp. red pepper flakes
2 cups half-and-half

1 cup low-sodium chicken broth
¼ cup fresh basil, chopped
1 cup grated reduced-fat Parmesan cheese
8 oz. ⅓-fat cream cheese
4 chicken breasts, cooked and diced
8 oz. high-fiber pasta, cooked

In a large skillet or saucepan over medium heat, add canola oil. Add green peppers, onion, and mushrooms. Sauté for 5-7 minutes.

Reduce heat to low and add red pepper flakes. Sauté for 2 minutes.

Add half-and-half and chicken broth. Simmer for 5 minutes.

Add basil, Parmesan cheese, and cream cheese. Stir until cheese is melted. Add diced chicken, and stir until warm. Serve over high-fiber pasta.

Yield: 8 servings

Nutrition Facts per Serving
Calories 350, Fat calories: 150, Total fat: 17 g, Saturated fat: 9 g, Cholesterol: 80 mg, Sodium: 350 mg, Total carbohydrates: 28 g, Dietary Fiber: 3 g, Sugar: 6 g, Protein: 20 g

Traditional Cajun Pasta Nutrition Facts per Serving
Calories: 1400, Total fat: 60 g, Total carbohydrates: 120 g

"Spice and Zing" Grilled Chicken

Tired of plain ol' grilled chicken? This dish is the answer to spicing up your next cookout. The marinade is as easy to make as it is tasty. I skinny-ed it by not only reducing the amount of oil but by preparing just enough marinade to coat the chicken. Marinate the chicken the morning of your event, and enjoy your guests instead of fussing in the kitchen.

2 tbsp. canola oil
¼ tsp. light Cajun seasoning
½ tsp. paprika

½ tsp. cayenne pepper
1 tsp. lemon pepper
4-6 skinless, boneless chicken breasts

In a large zip-top bag, combine oil, Cajun seasoning, paprika, cayenne pepper, and lemon pepper. Add chicken to bag. Seal, then toss to coat. Refrigerate for 2 hours.

Drain chicken and discard marinade. Place chicken on a hot grill and cook for 6-8 minutes per side. Serve.

Yield: 4-6 servings

Nutrition Facts per Serving
Calories: 160, Fat calories: 90, Total fat: 10 g, Saturated fat: 1 g, Cholesterol: 55 mg, Sodium: 310 mg, Total carbohydrates: 0 g, Dietary fiber: 0 g, Sugar: 0 g, Protein: 17 g

Cajun-Spiced Skinny Chicken Quesadillas

Need a quick and healthy supper? My Cajun-spiced skinny chicken quesadillas are incredibly simple and perfect for a weeknight dinner. This recipe is great for any chicken leftovers, and make sure to choose a high-fiber wrap (my favorite is the Mission Carb Balance Wrap).

½ lb. cooked chicken breast, chopped
½ red onion, sliced
1 green bell pepper, sliced
1 red bell pepper, sliced
¼ tsp. light Cajun seasoning
Nonstick cooking spray

4 large Mission Carb Balance Wraps (or any high-fiber wraps)
1 cup shredded mozzarella cheese
Light sour cream (optional)
Salsa (optional)

In a bowl, combine chicken, red onion, green pepper, red pepper, and Cajun seasoning.

Spray a large skillet with nonstick cooking spray. Lay 1 wrap in skillet over medium heat. Spoon ½ of chicken mixture on wrap. Sprinkle with ½ of cheese.

Top with a second tortilla. Cook for 1-3 minutes.

Carefully flip. Cook for 1-3 minutes. Remove from skillet.

Repeat with remaining wraps and fillings.

Cut each tortilla into 8 wedges. Serve with light sour cream and salsa, if desired.

Yield: 4 servings

Nutrition Facts per Serving
Calories: 250, Fat calories: 80, Total fat: 9 g, Saturated fat: 0.5 g, Cholesterol: 50 mg, Sodium: 630 mg, Total carbohydrates: 19 g, Dietary fiber: 11 g, Sugar: 3 g, Protein: 23 g

Traditional Chicken Quesadilla Nutrition Facts per Serving
Calories: 510, Total fat: 27 g, Saturated fat: 12 g, Cholesterol: 75 mg, Sodium: 1,190 mg, Total carbohydrates: 38 g, Dietary fiber: 4 g, Sugar 3 g

Crispy Oven-Fried Cajun Chicken

Fried chicken was a treat in my family, and as a little girl I would always pick the drumstick and chow down. I can still taste the hot, crispy skin . . . yummy. To this day, I love the taste, but I don't love the fat and calories. This recipe masters the famous fried chicken we Louisianans love without all the fat and calories. How did I skinny the traditional recipe? First, I used skinless chicken tenders. Instead of frying, I turned to the oven. However, the real secret is the coating. I lost the flour and used a combination of panko breadcrumbs and Fiber One Cereal to increase the fiber in the dish. This recipe is so yummy, you will think it is takeout!

2 cups water

1 tsp. light Cajun seasoning

12 (1-1½ lb.) chicken tenders

1 cup panko breadcrumbs, crushed

1 cup crushed Fiber One Cereal

1 tsp. black pepper

½ cup buttermilk

1 tsp. Tabasco pepper sauce

In a large container, pour water and Cajun seasoning. Add chicken. Cover and place in refrigerator for 4 hours.

Preheat oven to 350 degrees. Line a baking sheet with parchment paper.

In a large bowl, combine crushed panko bread crumbs, crushed Fiber One, and black pepper.

In a separate bowl, combine buttermilk and Tabasco.

Remove chicken from water mixture. Pat dry. Dredge chicken in panko mixture, shaking off excess.

Dip coated pieces into buttermilk. Allow excess to drip off.

Dredge again in panko mixture. Shake off excess.

Place on baking sheet. Bake for 40-45 minutes or until no longer pink in the center.

Yield: 6 servings

Nutrition Facts per Serving
Calories: 200, Fat calories: 30, Total fat: 3.5 g, Saturated fat: 1 g, Cholesterol: 75 mg, Sodium: 480 mg, Total carbohydrates: 18 g, Dietary fiber: 5 g, Sugar: 2 g, Protein: 27 g

Traditional Fried Chicken Nutrition Facts per Serving
Calories: 294, Total fat: 15 g, Saturated fat: 4 g, Cholesterol: 96 mg, Sodium: 311 mg, Total carbohydrates: 10 g, Dietary fiber: 0 g, Sugar: 0 g, Protein: 28 g

CRAWFISH

Crazy Good Crawfish Pizza

Did you know that 2 slices of pizza could have upwards of 520 calories? Pizza is a favorite in my house, and I always teach this skinny version to my clients. The secret is using a lower-carb wrap as a crust, replacing heavy cream with half-and-half, and letting the protein-rich, low-calorie crawfish shine. The result is a diabetic-friendly and incredibly tasty pizza.

4 large Mission Carb Balance Wraps
Nonstick cooking spray
1 tbsp. canola oil
1 cup half-and-half

¼ cup light sour cream
1 tsp. light Cajun seasoning
2 cups shredded mozzarella cheese
½ lb. crawfish tails, peeled and deveined

Preheat oven to 400 degrees. Line a baking sheet with parchment paper or aluminum foil.

Spray wraps with nonstick cooking spray. Lay 1 wrap on baking sheet. Bake for 1 minute. Repeat with remaining wraps.

In a medium saucepan, heat oil over medium-high heat. Stir in half-and-half and sour cream. Stir frequently. Bring to a boil, and stir for 5 minutes.

Add Cajun seasoning and stir. Remove from heat.

Lay 1 baked wrap on the baking sheet. Pour ¼ of sauce on wrap. Top with cheese and crawfish.

Bake for 10-15 minutes. Repeat with remaining ingredients.

Yield: 8 servings

Nutrition Facts per Serving
Calories: 310, Fat calories: 170, Total fat: 18 g, Saturated fat: 11 g, Cholesterol: 75 mg, Sodium: 670 mg, Total carbohydrates: 15 g, Dietary fiber: 5, Sugar: 2 g, Protein 23 g

Traditional Pepperoni Pizza Nutrition Facts per Serving
Calories: 580, Total fat: 24 g, Total carbohydrates: 65 g

Colossal Crawfish and Cauliflower Casserole

Many casserole dishes contain over a stick of butter and loads of full-fat cream cheese. How can we skinny this Southern staple? A few substitutions take this dish from "no thanks" to "yes please." I switched from butter and full-fat cream cheese to heart-healthy olive oil and light cream cheese. The real secret is using cauliflower as the "starch," which helps to reduce the amount of carbs in the dish. The result is a creamy, delicious casserole worthy of your next potluck gathering.

Nonstick cooking spray
1 pkg. frozen steam-in-the-bag cauliflower
2 tbsp. olive oil
1 onion, chopped
1 green bell pepper, chopped

1 cup sliced mushrooms
8 oz. ⅓-fat cream cheese
1 lb. crawfish tails, peeled and deveined
1 tsp. light Cajun seasoning

Preheat oven to 350 degrees. Spray a 9x13 baking pan with nonstick cooking spray.

Microwave cauliflower for 1 minute less than recommended pkg. directions. Remove from microwave and chop cauliflower. Set aside.

In a large skillet, heat olive oil over medium heat. Add onion, bell pepper, and mushrooms. Sauté for 5-7 minutes.

Add cream cheese. Stir until melted. Add crawfish tails and Cajun seasoning and stir. Stir in cooked cauliflower.

Pour mixture into baking pan. Bake for 20-25 minutes.

Yield: 8 servings

Nutrition Facts per Serving
Calories: 150, Fat calories: 80, Total fat: 10 g, Saturated fat: 4 g, Cholesterol: 80 mg, Sodium: 240 mg, Total carbohydrates: 4 g, Dietary fiber: 2 g, Sugar: 2 g, Protein: 11 g

Traditional Crawfish Casserole Nutrition Facts per Serving
Calories: 385, Total fat: 18 g, Sodium: 953 mg, Total carbohydrates: 37 g, Sugar: 2 g

Second Line Crawfish Casserole

It was difficult selecting my favorite crawfish casserole for this book, so I decided to share two with you! If you are looking for a creamier choice, this will be your new preferred casserole. I skinny-ed this recipe in the traditional fashion by replacing some of the rice with the superstar cauliflower and using the pantry-friendly staple of a lower-fat cream soup. Grab your umbrella and dance!

Nonstick cooking spray
1 pkg. frozen steam-in-the-bag cauliflower
1 lb. crawfish tails, peeled and deveined
2 cans Healthy Request or 98 percent fat-free cream of mushroom soup
1 can diced tomatoes
½ cup rice, cooked

1 onion, chopped
1 green bell pepper, chopped
3 stalks celery, chopped
⅓ cup parsley, chopped
1 tsp. light Cajun seasoning
½ tsp. cayenne pepper
1½ cups shredded 2 percent cheddar cheese

Preheat oven to 350 degrees. Spray a 3-qt. casserole dish with nonstick cooking spray.

Microwave cauliflower for 1 minute less than recommended pkg. directions. Remove from microwave and chop cauliflower.

In a large bowl, combine cooked cauliflower, crawfish, soup, diced tomatoes, rice, onion, green pepper, celery, parsley, Cajun seasoning, and cayenne pepper. Pour mixture into prepared casserole dish. Cover and bake for 45 minutes.

Uncover and sprinkle with cheese. Return to oven and bake uncovered for 15 minutes.

Yield: **10 servings**

Nutrition Facts per Serving
Calories: 140, Fat calories: 45, Total fat: 5 g, Saturated fat: 2.5 g, Cholesterol: 60 mg, Sodium: 400 mg, Total carbohydrates: 11 g, Dietary fiber: 2 g, Sugar: 3 g, Protein: 12 g

Traditional Crawfish Casserole Nutrition Facts per Serving
Calories: 385, Total fat: 18 g, Sodium: 953 mg, Total carbohydrates: 37 g, Sugar: 2 g

Christian's Fave Crawfish Rice Dressing

I love a rice dressing. The meat and rice are a match made in foodie heaven. But what I don't love is the high carb count. In order to make this dish more diabetic friendly and health conscious, I used my famous substitution—cauliflower. It sounds odd, but I promise you will not miss the double portion of rice. Just ask my son Christian, because this is his favorite Skinny Louisiana dish!

Nonstick cooking spray
1 pkg. frozen steam-in-the-bag cauliflower
1 lb. 90 percent lean ground sirloin
1 onion, chopped
3 stalks celery, chopped
1 green bell pepper, chopped
1 red bell pepper, chopped

½ cup rice, cooked
1 lb. crawfish tails, peeled and deveined
1 cup chopped pecans
1 tbsp. canola oil
1 tsp. light Cajun seasoning
½ tsp. cayenne pepper
1 tsp. black pepper

Preheat oven to 350 degrees. Spray a 9x13 baking pan with nonstick cooking spray.

Microwave cauliflower for 1 minute less than recommended pkg. directions. Remove from microwave and chop cauliflower. Set aside.

In a large skillet or saucepan over medium-high heat, cook ground sirloin, onion, celery, green pepper, and red pepper for 5-7 minutes or until meat is no longer pink.

Stir in rice, cauliflower, crawfish, pecans, canola oil, Cajun seasoning, cayenne pepper, and black pepper. Cook for 3 minutes.

Transfer mixture to baking pan. Bake for 25 minutes.

Yield: **10 servings**

Serving Size: **1 cup**

Nutrition Facts per Serving
Calories: 230, Fat calories: 130, Total fat: 14 g, Saturated fat: 2.5 g, Cholesterol: 80 mg, Sodium: 140 mg, Total carbohydrates: 7 g, Dietary fiber: 3 g, Sugar: 3 g, Protein: 18 g

Traditional Crawfish Dressing Nutrition Facts per Serving
Calories: 410, Total fat: 15 g, Saturated fat: 4 g, Sodium: 640 mg, Total carbohydrates: 47 g, Sugar: 8 g

Pizzazz and Jazz Crawfish Quesadillas

I am always looking for a quick dinner entree full of flavor and pizzazz. Enter these amazing crawfish quesadillas. Crawfish are astonishingly low in calories yet pack a protein punch, making them a perfect addition to the Skinny Louisiana lifestyle. The high-fiber wraps result in diabetic-friendly quesadillas.

1 lb. crawfish tails, peeled and deveined
½ onion, sliced
1 green bell pepper, sliced
1 red bell pepper, sliced
¼ tsp. light taco seasoning
¼ tsp. light Cajun seasoning

Nonstick cooking spray
4 large Mission Carb Balance Wraps
1 cup shredded mozzarella cheese
¼ cup cilantro, chopped
Light sour cream

In a bowl, combine crawfish, onion, green pepper, red pepper, taco seasoning, and Cajun seasoning.

Spray a large skillet with nonstick cooking spray. Over medium heat, add 1 wrap. Layer ¼ of crawfish mixture on wrap. Sprinkle with ¼ of cheese.

Fold over wrap. Cook for 1-3 minutes.

Carefully flip. Cook for 1-3 minutes.

Remove from skillet. Repeat steps with remaining wraps and fillings.

Cut each wrap into 4 wedges. Serve with cilantro and light sour cream.

Yield: 4 servings

Nutrition Facts per Serving
Calories: 301, Fat calories: 90, Total fat: 10 g, Saturated fat: 5 g, Cholesterol: 135 mg, Sodium: 670 mg, Total carbohydrates: 24 g, Dietary fiber: 12 g, Sugar: 4 g, Protein: 30 g

SHRIMP

Radiant Rosemary-Lemon Shrimp

Rosemary-lemon shrimp is a common appetizer at many restaurants and is served alone, on skewers, or as a topping on a salad. Shrimp is an amazing source of protein, and while this dish has remarkable skinny properties, they can be easily destroyed by using too much butter or oil. My goal here was simplicity. I used just enough heart-healthy olive oil and focused on the flavors of rosemary and lemon. The result is a protein-rich, low-carb, 5-ingredient shrimp dish that welcomes in spring.

2 tbsp. olive oil
10-12 oz. large raw shrimp, peeled and
    deveined

3 tbsp. lemon juice
3 tbsp. chopped rosemary
1 tsp. black pepper

In a large saucepan, heat olive oil over medium-high heat. Add shrimp. Cook for 5-7 minutes or until shrimp are opaque.

Add lemon juice and rosemary. Cook for 1-2 minutes.

Reduce heat to low. Add pepper and stir. Cook for 30 seconds. Serve.

Yield: 4 servings

Nutrition Facts per Serving
Calories: 160, Fat calories: 80, Total fat: 8 g, Saturated fat: 1 g, Cholesterol: 130 mg, Sodium: 130 mg, Total carbohydrates: 2 g, Dietary fiber: 0 g, Sugar: 0 g, Protein: 17 g

Spicy Baked Shrimp

Many of our favorite shrimp dishes are served with a buttery sauce and French bread. These taste amazing, but the calories, fat, and carbs from the sauce and bread are not heart healthy. Here I focus on the star of the dish—shrimp. This low-calorie protein, combined with amazing spices and flavorings, will make your heart sing.

1 tbsp. olive oil
2 tbsp. chili sauce
1 tbsp. Worcestershire sauce
1 tsp. paprika
½ tsp. Tabasco or pepper sauce

1 tsp. lemon juice
2 tbsp. parsley, chopped
2 tbsp. water
1 lb. medium shrimp, peeled and deveined

Preheat oven to 400 degrees.

In a small saucepan, heat olive oil over medium-high heat. Add chili sauce, Worcestershire, paprika, Tabasco, lemon juice, parsley, and water. Bring to a boil.

Reduce heat to low. Cook for 10 minutes.

Place shrimp in a medium-size casserole dish. Pour spice mixture over shrimp. Bake for 15-20 minutes.

Yield: 4 servings

Nutrition Facts per Serving
Calories: 160, Fat calories: 50, Total fat: 5 g, Saturated fat: 0 g, Cholesterol: 170 mg, Sodium: 340 mg, Total carbohydrates: 4 g, Dietary fiber: 0 g, Sugar: 2 g, Protein: 23 g

Cheerful Cajun Spinach and Shrimp Pasta Sauce

While I adore a bowl of creamy fettuccine alfredo, I don't adore the fat, calories, and carbs that come with it. I skinny-ed this dish by replacing the heavy cream with half-and-half and using a reduced-fat Parmesan cheese. While this sauce is an amazing makeover of the original, we can easily make the mistake of consuming too much pasta. Be sure to look for a whole-grain pasta with 5 grams of fiber or higher per serving.

1 tbsp. olive oil
1 lb. shrimp, peeled and deveined
2 garlic cloves, minced
1 cup half-and-half

½ cup grated reduced-fat Parmesan cheese
2 tsp. light Cajun seasoning
2 cups spinach

In a large saucepan, heat olive oil over medium heat. Add shrimp. Cook for 5-7 minutes or until shrimp are opaque.

Add garlic. Cook for 1 minute.

Pour in half-and-half. Stir. Sprinkle in Parmesan cheese and stir. Mix in Cajun seasoning.

Reduce heat to medium low. Stir in spinach. Stir constantly, making sure sauce does not boil, until spinach wilts. Serve over high-fiber pasta.

Yield: 6-8 servings

Sauce Nutrition Facts per Serving
Calories: 270, Fat calories: 15, Total fat: 6 g, Saturated fat: 0 g, Cholesterol: 205 mg, Sodium: 660 mg, Total carbohydrates: 5 g, Dietary fiber: 0 g, Sugar: 3 g, Protein: 28 g

SLiMMed-DOWN CreaMy SeaFood Pasta

With some simple substitutions, we are able to enjoy this delicious dish without the guilt! I reduced the carbs by over 30 percent by using only 1 tbsp. all-purpose flour instead of the traditional ¹/₂ cup. I also saved fat by decreasing the oil from ¹/₄ cup to 2 tbsp. and switching from cream to half-and-half. The result? This creamy seafood pasta is an excellent source of protein and a slimmed-down version of a favorite sauce. Remember to ladle it over a pasta with 5 grams of fiber or higher per serving.

2 tbsp. canola oil
1 lb. raw shrimp, peeled and deveined
1 lb. crawfish tails, peeled and deveined
½ onion, minced
1 garlic clove, minced
1 tbsp. all-purpose flour
1 can (14.5 oz.) diced tomatoes
½ cup chopped basil

1 cup half-and-half
½ cup reduced-sodium chicken broth
1 tbsp. tomato paste
½ tsp. light Cajun seasoning
½ cup shredded reduced-fat Parmesan cheese
8 oz. high-fiber pasta, cooked

In a large skillet, heat 1 tbsp. canola oil over medium-high heat. Add shrimp and crawfish. Cook for 5-7 minutes or until shrimp are pink. Drain liquid. Set crawfish and shrimp aside.

Add remaining 1 tbsp. canola oil to skillet. Add onion and garlic. Cook for 3 minutes.

Add flour. Cook for 1-2 minutes while constantly stirring mixture.

Stir in tomatoes and basil. Cook for 5-7 minutes.

Stir in half-and-half, reduced-sodium chicken broth, tomato paste, and Cajun seasoning. Reduce heat to low. Cook for 5-7 minutes.

Add cheese, shrimp, and crawfish. Stir until all meat is warm. Serve over high-fiber pasta.

Yield: **8 servings**

Nutrition Facts per Serving
Calories: 210, Fat calories: 90, Total fat: 10 g, Saturated fat: 3.5 g, Cholesterol: 165 mg, Sodium: 400 mg, Total carbohydrates: 7 g, Dietary fiber: 1 g, Sugar: 3 g, Protein: 23 g

It's Great Garlic Shrimp

While traditional versions of garlic shrimp grace the appetizer menus of many restaurants, these dishes are often served with a slice of crusty French bread, yielding a high-carbohydrate meal. In this tasty, skinny recipe, I lose the bread and switch out the butter for heart-healthy olive oil. Trust me, you won't miss the bread!

2 tbsp. olive oil	1 lemon, cut into small wedges
1 tsp. chopped garlic	2 bay leaves
½ onion, chopped	1 lb. shrimp, peeled and deveined

In a large saucepan, heat olive oil over medium heat. Add garlic, onion, lemon, and bay leaves. Sauté for 3 minutes.

Add shrimp. Stir and cover. Cook for 5-7 minutes or until no longer pink.

Remove pan from heat. Let stand for 15 minutes. Serve.

Yield: 6 servings

Nutrition Facts per Serving
Calories: 190, Fat calories: 80, Total fat: 9 g, Saturated fat: 1 g, Cholesterol: 170 mg, Sodium: 170 mg, Total carbohydrates: less than 1 g, Dietary fiber: less than 1 g, Sugar: less than 1 g, Protein: 24 g

Sizzling and Spicy Shrimp

While a 3-oz. serving of shrimp is only 90 calories and an amazing source of protein, we tend to destroy this coastal gift with tons of butter and salt. As in my other recipes, I focused here on flavor, not fat and sodium. The result is a spicy version of a favorite seafood dish that can be prepared for a quick weeknight meal.

1 lb. shrimp, peeled and deveined
1 tbsp. olive oil
½ tbsp. adobo sauce

1 tsp. light Cajun seasoning
1 tsp. honey

In a large bowl, mix all ingredients. In a medium skillet over medium-high heat, cook mixture for 5-7 or until shrimp are opaque. Serve.

Yield: 4 servings

Nutrition Facts per Serving
Calories: 160, Fat calories: 50, Total fat: 6 g, Saturated fat: 0 g, Cholesterol: 170 mg, Sodium: 290 mg, Total carbohydrates: 3 g, Dietary fiber: 0 g, Sugar: 2 g, Protein: 23 g

Skinny New Orleans Barbecue Shrimp

While the traditional version is a wonderful break from fried seafood dishes, I still had a little work to do to give this recipe a full skinny twist. I used a much lower amount of olive oil, a reduced-sodium beef broth in place of the beer, Tabasco instead of salt, and no French bread. I changed the spices to suit my palate and developed an incredible skinny twist you are sure to love! In fact, this recipe is so yummy, Men's Fitness *named it one of the 50 Healthiest Recipes Known to Man.*

¼ cup olive oil
1 tbsp. chopped rosemary
1 tsp. black pepper
2 tsp. light Cajun seasoning
2 garlic cloves, minced

2 tbsp. Worcestershire sauce
2 tbsp. Tabasco pepper sauce
2 tbsp. lemon juice
2 lb. shrimp, peeled and deveined
1 cup reduced-sodium beef broth

In a large skillet, heat olive oil over medium heat. Add rosemary, pepper, Cajun seasoning, and garlic. Cook for 1-2 minutes.

Add Worcestershire sauce, Tabasco sauce, lemon juice, and shrimp. Cook for 5-7 minutes or until shrimp are pink.

Add beef broth. Cook for 2-3 additional minutes. Serve.

Yield: 8 servings

Serving Size: 11 shrimp

Nutrition Facts per Serving
Calories: 190, Fat calories: 80, Total fat: 9 g, Saturated fat: 1 g, Cholesterol: 170 mg, Sodium: 420 mg, Total carbohydrates: 3 g, Dietary fiber: 0 g, Sugar: less than 1 g, Protein: 24 g

Traditional Barbecue Shrimp Nutrition Facts per Serving
Calories: 690, Total fat: 50.2 g, Sodium: 944 mg, Total carbohydrates: 9.6 g, Sugar: 0 g

SKINNY SHRIMP Tacos

When we include protein-rich shrimp in our taco night, we have a great meal the entire family will enjoy. Unfortunately, the crispy taco shells and full-fat sour cream can add calories, carbs, and fat. My skinny solutions? I sautéed the shrimp in only 1 tbsp. olive oil and switched the optional topping to light sour cream. I also used high-fiber wraps (5 grams of fiber or higher) instead of crispy taco shells. This recipe is so easy and tasty that BuzzFeed featured it in "Here's What Real Healthy People Actually Eat for Lunch."

1 tbsp. olive oil
½ cup chopped onion
12-16 oz. shrimp, peeled and deveined
¼ cup lime juice
1 tsp. chili powder
1 tsp. light Cajun seasoning

8 Mission Carb Balance Wraps
½ red cabbage, shredded
½ green cabbage, shredded
1 cup cilantro, chopped
Light sour cream (optional)

In a large saucepan or skillet, heat olive oil over medium heat. Add onion. Cook for 3-5 minutes or until onion is soft.

Add shrimp. Cook for 5-7 minutes or until shrimp are pink and opaque.

Reduce heat to low. Add lime juice, chili powder, and Cajun seasoning. Cook for 1-2 minutes.

Fill wraps with shrimp, cabbage, and cilantro. Add sour cream if desired. Enjoy!

Yield: 8 tacos

Nutrition Facts per Serving*
Calories: 120, Fat calories: 35, Total fat: 4 g, Saturated fat: 1 g, Cholesterol: 70 mg, Sodium: 200 mg, Total carbohydrates: 10 g, Dietary fiber: 3 g, Sugar: 4 g, Protein: 11 g

*Nutrition facts were not calculated using Mission Carb Balance Wraps.

Smashing Shrimp and Ham Cauliflower Grits

Shrimp and grits are the ultimate Southern comfort food. We love the taste but not the calories, fat, carbs, and sodium. Believe it or not, skinny-ing this dish was not difficult. First I reduced the amount of oil, eliminated the salt, and used reduced-sodium chicken broth and 2 percent milk. I continued by replacing the heavy cream with half-and-half and including low-sodium ham. The most shocking change comes from using cauliflower. Don't worry; I still have grits in the dish, but just a smaller amount, making it a must-have for our diabetic population. Keep preparation simple and quick by purchasing steam-in-the-bag cauliflower in the freezer section of your local supermarket.

1 tbsp. canola oil
1 lb. shrimp, peeled and deveined
½ tsp. light Cajun seasoning
1 cup chopped low-sodium ham
1 onion, chopped
1 green bell pepper, minced
1 garlic clove, chopped
1 cup reduced-sodium chicken broth
½ cup half-and-half

GRITS
1 pkg. frozen steam-in-the-bag cauliflower
3 cups water
¾ cup quick-cooking grits
2 cups 2 percent milk
1 cup half-and-half
1 tbsp. canola oil

In a large saucepan over medium heat, cook oil, shrimp, Cajun seasoning, and ham for 5-7 minutes or until shrimp are no longer pink. Remove from pan.

Add onion and green pepper to pan. Cook for 5-7 minutes.

Add garlic. Cook for 1 minute.

Add broth and stir. Cook for 5 minutes.

Stir in half-and-half. Pour into shrimp mixture. Set aside.

Microwave cauliflower for 1 minute less than recommended pkg. directions. Remove from microwave and chop cauliflower. Set aside.

In a medium saucepan, bring the water to a boil.

Add grits and stir. When grits thicken, add milk, half-and-half, chopped cauliflower, and canola oil. Return to a boil.

Reduce heat to a simmer and cook for 45 minutes to 1 hour.

Ladle cauliflower grits into bowls. Ladle shrimp mixture over cauliflower grits.

Yield: 8 servings

Nutrition Facts per Serving
Calories: 260, Fat calories: 120, Total fat: 13 g, Saturated fat: 5 g, Cholesterol: 125 mg, Sodium: 600 mg, Total carbohydrates: 11 g, Dietary Fiber: 1 g, Sugar: 7 g, Protein: 23 g

Desserts

SKiNNy LouiSiaNa StraWberry CobbLer

Despite the April heat, many flock to the Ponchatoula Strawberry Festival for fun and tasty strawberry dishes. What's not to love about the strawberry? One cup contains only 45 calories and packs a punch of 3 grams of fiber. I skinny-ed this recipe by replacing half the sugar with applesauce and added a great crunch with crushed Fiber One Cereal, making this dessert perfect for any holiday gathering.

Nonstick cooking spray
2 pt. Louisiana strawberries, quartered
2 tbsp. sugar
2 tbsp. applesauce
¼ cup brown sugar

½ cup quick-cooking oats
¼ cup crushed Fiber One Cereal
1 tbsp. all-purpose flour
1 tbsp. butter, softened
Light whipped topping

Preheat oven to 350 degrees. Spray a 3-qt. casserole dish with nonstick cooking spray. Combine strawberries, sugar, and applesauce in casserole dish.

In a separate bowl, combine brown sugar, oats, crushed Fiber One, flour, and butter. Blend with a fork. Pour topping over strawberry mixture. Spray topping with nonstick cooking spray.

Bake for 30 minutes. Remove dish from oven.

Let stand for 10-15 minutes. Serve with light whipped topping.

Yield: *8 servings*

Nutrition Facts per Serving
Calories: 100, Fat calories: 20, Total fat: 2 g, Saturated fat: 1 g, Cholesterol: less than 5 mg, Sodium: 0 mg, Total carbohydrates: 21 g, Dietary fiber: 3 g, Sugar: 14 g, Protein: 1 g

Traditional Strawberry Cobbler Nutrition Facts per Serving
Calories: 663, Total fat: 31 g, Total carbohydrates: 89 g

Sassy Strawberry Oat Bars

When I am craving something sweet but not chocolate, I always reach for these bars. How did I skinny this dish? I punched up the fiber by using oats and Fiber One Cereal and decreased calories by replacing half the sugar with applesauce. I also am introducing you to two new secrets. I replaced half the butter with plain nonfat Greek yogurt and found a sugar-free, high-fiber preserve (Polaner) to decrease calories even more. These bars will make you throw away your prepackaged fruit bars in a hurry.

1½ cups rolled oats
½ cup all-purpose flour
¼ cup crushed Fiber One Cereal
¼ cup sugar
¼ cup applesauce
2 tsp. lemon zest
½ tsp. baking powder

¼ tsp. salt
½ cup plain nonfat Greek yogurt
¼ cup butter
1 pt. Louisiana strawberries, quartered
½ cup Polaner Sugar Free with Fiber
 Strawberry Preserves
2 tsp. vanilla extract

Preheat oven to 375 degrees. Line an 8x8 baking pan with nonstick foil or parchment paper.

In a large bowl, combine oats, flour, Fiber One Cereal, sugar, applesauce, lemon zest, baking powder, and salt. Add Greek yogurt and butter. Combine with a fork until the mixture forms a crumbly dough.

Press ⅔ of the dough on the bottom of the lined pan. Bake for 15-20 minutes or until the edges start to brown.

In a separate medium bowl, combine quartered strawberries, high-fiber preserves, and vanilla. Spread mixture over baked crust. Sprinkle remaining crumbs over strawberry mixture. Bake for 20-25 minutes.

Cool. Refrigerate for 1-2 hours. Cut into bars.

Yield: **16 bars**

Nutrition Facts per Serving
Calories: 100, Fat calories: 30, Total fat: 3.5 g, Saturated fat: 2 g, Cholesterol: 10 mg, Sodium: 65 mg, Total carbohydrates: 16 g, Dietary fiber: 3 g, Sugar: 5 g, Protein: 2 g

Traditional Strawberry Bars Nutrition Facts per Serving
Calories: 297, Total fat: 11 g, Sodium: 75 mg, Total carbohydrates: 46 g

Strawberry Pizza Bites

While most of us envision pizza as a greasy fast-food treat, switch your thinking and try this strawberry version. To skinny it, I eliminated all sugar and focused on the flavor of the strawberry, and instead of a high-fat crust, I used Flatout Flatbread. Quick, easy, and sweet? Sign me up!

2 Flatout Flatbreads or other high-fiber wrap (5 g fiber or more)
Nonstick cooking spray
2 cups chopped strawberries
¼ cup basil, chopped

1 tbsp. honey
1 tbsp. vanilla extract
¼ tsp. cinnamon
4 oz. light cream cheese, softened

Preheat oven to 400 degrees. Line a baking sheet with nonstick foil or parchment paper.

Cut Flatout breads into squares. Spray each side with nonstick cooking spray. Bake for 4 minutes. Flip and bake for 4 minutes. Remove from oven and cool.

In a medium bowl, combine strawberries, basil, honey, vanilla, and cinnamon.

Spread cream cheese on bread squares. Top with strawberry mixture. Serve.

Yield: 4 servings

Nutrition Facts per Serving
Calories: 170, Fat calories: 70, Total fat: 7 g, Saturated fat: 3.5 g, Cholesterol: 20 mg, Sodium: 210 mg, Total carbohydrates: 20 g, Dietary fiber: 6 g, Sugar: 10 g, Protein: 7 g

Traditional Strawberry Pizza Nutrition Facts per Serving
Calories: 238, Total fat: 10 g, Sodium: 177 mg, Total carbohydrates: 36 g

PerFectLy SLiM PuMPKiN PiE DiP

A pumpkin obsession exists in my Skinny Louisiana house. My husband loves anything pumpkin, and he passed this lovely passion on to our two kids. While I do enjoy a pumpkin-spice latte, I don't like the 400 calories in this seasonal beverage. I wondered how I could skinny this popular drink. I also craved a healthier alternative to pumpkin cheesecake. My answer? I left the high-calorie beverage behind and focused on a cheesecake-type filling without the crust. Voila: a yummy, skinny dip! I saved hundreds of calories without losing flavor by using light cream cheese and exchanging half the sugar for marshmallow fluff. Pumpkin is a star that can stand in for butter in many desserts. You will be sold on this delicious dip!

8 oz. light cream cheese, softened
⅓ cup powdered sugar
⅓ cup marshmallow fluff

1 can 100 percent pumpkin pie filling
1 tsp. pumpkin spice

In a medium bowl, beat cream cheese for 1 minute.

Add powdered sugar and marshmallow fluff. Beat for 1 minute.

Add pumpkin pie filling and pumpkin spice. Beat for 1 minute. Serve with apple slices, vanilla wafers, or graham crackers.

Yield: *About 2½ cups*

Serving Size: *2 tbsp.*

Nutrition Facts per Serving
Calories: 50, Fat calories: 25, Total fat: 2.5 g, Saturated fat: 2.5 g, Cholesterol: 10 mg, Sodium: 50 mg, Total carbohydrates: 5 g, Dietary fiber: 4 g, Sugar: 3 g, Protein: 1 g

Traditional Pumpkin Cheesecake Nutrition Facts per Serving
Calories: 739, Total fat: 47 g, Sodium: 500 mg, Total carbohydrates: 68 g

So-Slim Sweet Potato Pie Dip

Gorgeous, tasty, and healthy—it's no wonder the sweet potato is a popular choice for our holiday celebrations. One medium sweet potato is only 130 calories and serves as an amazing source of vitamin A, which is needed for great skin and eyes. However, 1 slice of our beloved sweet potato pie can have 340 calories. I got rid of the high-carb crust and transformed the pie into a dip. In addition, I used oil instead of butter and applesauce in place of most of the oil and sugar, reducing fat and saving hundreds of calories. The result is deliciousness!

Nonstick cooking spray
8 oz. light cream cheese, softened
½ cup brown sugar
⅔ cup applesauce
2 sweet potatoes, peeled, cooked, and
  mashed
1 tsp. canola oil
1 tbsp. vanilla extract

1 tsp. cinnamon
¼ tsp. nutmeg

TOPPING
½ cup chopped pecans
1 tbsp. sugar
1 tbsp. brown sugar
1 tbsp. canola oil

Preheat oven to 350 degrees. Spray a 9-inch pie dish with nonstick cooking spray.

In a medium bowl, beat cream cheese and brown sugar for 1 minute.

Stir in applesauce, mashed sweet potatoes, canola oil, vanilla, cinnamon, and nutmeg. When well combined, pour mixture into pie dish.

To prepare topping, in a separate small bowl, mix pecans, sugar, brown sugar, and canola oil. Layer pecan mixture over pie. Bake for 15-20 minutes. Serve with graham crackers and apple slices.

Yield: About 4½ cups

Serving Size: 2 tbsp.

Nutrition Facts per Serving
Calories: 80, Fat calories: 30, Total fat: 3.5 g, Saturated fat: 0 g, Cholesterol: 0 mg, Sodium: 15 mg, Total carbohydrates: 12 g, Dietary fiber: 1 g, Sugar: 9 g, Protein: 1 g

Traditional Restaurant Sweet Potato Pie Nutrition Facts per Serving
Calories: 340, Total fat: 17 g, Sodium: 240 mg, Total carbohydrates: 44 g

Marry Me Peppermint Cheesecake Dip

Peppermint tingles the taste buds, and this dip brings feelings of love and happiness to everyone around. I call this dish "Marry Me" since it was such a hit at a bachelorette party, and I promise it will be a smash at any celebration you might be planning. Is it skinny? Just check out the calorie savings below!

8 oz. light cream cheese, softened
1 cup marshmallow fluff
1 tbsp. vanilla extract

½ cup crushed peppermints
¼ cup miniature dark chocolate chips

In a medium bowl, beat cream cheese for 2 minutes.

Add marshmallow fluff and vanilla. Beat for 1 minute.

Stir in peppermint and dark chocolate chips. Serve with graham crackers or apple slices.

Yield: About 2½ cups

Serving Size: 2 tbsp.

Nutrition Facts per Serving
Calories: 60, Fat calories: 15, Total fat: 1.5 g, Saturated fat: 1 g, Cholesterol: 0 mg, Sodium: 10 mg, Total carbohydrates: 13 g, Dietary fiber: 0 g, Sugar: 10 mg, Protein: 0 g

Cheesecake Factory Peppermint Cheesecake Nutrition Facts per Serving
Calories: 900, Total fat: 35 g, Sodium: 410, Total carbohydrates: 91 g

King Cake Cheesecake Bites

Every year starting January 6, king cakes are proudly displayed at our grocery stores. I decided to take the plunge and develop a skinnier version of this classic. What better flavors to merge than king cake and cheesecake? I skinny-ed this recipe by using a light cream cheese as well as much less sugar than traditional cheesecakes include. The result? Say hello to your new favorite Mardi Gras dish.

¾ cup crushed graham crackers
2 tsp. canola oil
16 oz. light cream cheese, softened
2 eggs
⅓ cup sugar
⅓ cup applesauce

1 tbsp. vanilla extract
1 tbsp. powdered sugar
½ tsp. milk
¼ tsp. almond extract
1 tbsp. sugar
Green, yellow, and purple food coloring

Preheat oven to 375 degrees. Line a 9x13 baking pan with parchment paper.

In a medium bowl, combine graham cracker crumbs and oil. Press into the pan.

In a separate medium bowl, combine cream cheese, eggs, sugar, applesauce, and vanilla extract. Beat for 2 minutes.

Pour mixture into pan. Bake for 20 minutes. Cool.

In a small bowl, combine powdered sugar, milk, and almond extract. Set aside.

In 3 zip-top bags, place 1 tsp. sugar each. Add 1 drop food coloring to each bag, using a different color for each. Shake.

Drizzle sugar glaze over cheesecake. Sprinkle with colored sugar. Cut into squares.

Yield: 24 squares

Nutrition Facts per Serving
Calories: 90, Fat calories: 50, Total fat: 6 g, Saturated fat: 2.5 g, Cholesterol: 30 mg, Sodium: 100 mg, Total carbohydrates: 7 g, Dietary Fiber: 0 g, Sugar: 5 g, Protein: 2 g

Cheesecake Factory Cheesecake Nutrition Facts per Serving
Calories: 710, Total fat: 29 g, Sodium: 430 mg, Total carbohydrates: 62 g

S'Mores Brownie Bars

What if you could bring the amazing messiness and deliciousness of a s'more to a bar? I did! To skinny this, I dropped the butter and halved the sugar and marshmallows, reducing fat and calories, as well as added All-Bran Bran Buds Cereal for some fiber. Be sure to use a dark chocolate candy bar, since its sugar count is lower than milk chocolate. I promise, this will bring you back to your camping days.

2 tbsp. canola oil
½ cup sugar
½ cup applesauce
1 egg
2 tsp. vanilla extract
1 cup flour

⅓ cup All-Bran Bran Buds Cereal
4 sheets graham crackers, crushed
1 tsp. baking powder
¼ tsp. salt
4 fun-size dark chocolate candy bars
2 cups miniature marshmallows

Preheat oven to 350 degrees. Line a 9x13 baking pan with parchment paper or aluminum foil.

In a medium bowl, beat oil, sugar, and applesauce for 30 seconds.

Add egg and vanilla. Beat for 30 seconds.

In a separate bowl, combine flour, All-Bran Bran Buds, graham cracker crumbs, baking powder, and salt. Add applesauce mixture. Beat until well blended.

Press mixture into bottom of pan. Bake for 15 minutes.

Break up candy bars. Layer chocolate pieces over baked layer. Sprinkle marshmallows over chocolate.

Bake for 10-15 minutes. Cool.

Cut and serve.

Yield: **24 bars**

Nutrition Facts per Serving
Calories: 100, Fat calories: 30, Total fat: 3.5 g, Saturated fat: 1 g, Cholesterol: 10 mg, Sodium: 50 mg, Total carbohydrates: 18 g, Dietary fiber: 1 g, Sugar: 11 g, Protein: 1 g

Traditional S'mores Brownie Nutrition Facts per Serving
Calories: 251, Total fat: 11 g, Sodium: 459 mg, Total carbohydrates: 24 g

Simply Amazing Skinny Creole Brownies

These brownies have a special ingredient—coffee with chicory! Also, many of us don't realize that cocoa is low in sugar. In traditional skinny fashion, I replaced half the sugar with applesauce and increased the fiber by replacing half the flour with oats. This dessert is simply amazing.

2 tbsp. canola oil
1 cup applesauce
½ tsp. salt
1 cup cocoa
1 cup sugar
1 tbsp. vanilla extract
3 eggs
½ cup all-purpose flour
½ cup oat flour or ground oats
½ tsp. baking powder

¼ cup mini dark chocolate chips

GANACHE
2 tbsp. fat-free half-and-half
1 tbsp. canola oil
1 tbsp. sugar
Dash of salt
2 tbsp. dark chocolate chips
2 tbsp. brewed coffee with chicory
¼ tsp. vanilla extract

Preheat oven to 350 degrees. Line a 9x13 baking pan with parchment paper or aluminum foil.

In a small saucepan over low heat, combine canola oil, applesauce, salt, and cocoa. Stir until melted and smooth. Remove from heat.

In a medium bowl, combine sugar, vanilla extract, eggs, flour, oat flour, and baking powder. Pour cocoa mixture into flour mixture. Beat for 2-3 minutes. Stir in mini dark chocolate chips.

Pour batter into baking pan. Bake for 20-25 minutes. Cool.

To make ganache, in a small saucepan over very low heat, add half-and-half, canola oil, sugar, and salt. Stir until combined.

Add dark chocolate chips. Stir until chocolate is melted. Remove from heat.

Add coffee and vanilla. Stir. Pour ganache over brownies. Cut into squares.

Yield: 24 squares

Nutrition Facts per Servings
Calories: 150, Fat Calories: 40, Total fat: 4.5 g, Saturated fat: 1.5 g, Cholesterol: 25 mg, Sodium: 75 mg, Total carbohydrates: 27 g, Dietary fiber: 2 g, Sugar: 20 g, Protein: 2 g

Traditional Brownie Nutrition Facts per Serving
Calories: 405, Total fat: 27, Sodium: 130 mg, Total carbohydrates: 43 g

Skinny Root-Beer Bars

Nothing is better on a hot, humid Louisiana day than a root-beer float. My grandmother made root beer from scratch, and to this day it is my favorite summer drink. While I love a float, I don't love the calories. I transformed the taste into this yummy bar with some simple skinny substitutes.

Nonstick cooking spray
1 cup chopped pecans
¾ cup all-purpose flour
¼ cup Fiber One Cereal, crushed
¼ tsp. baking powder
⅛ tsp. baking soda
⅛ tsp. salt

2 tbsp. canola oil
⅔ cup applesauce
⅓ cup brown sugar
3 tbsp. honey
2 eggs
1½ tsp. root-beer concentrate
1 tsp. vanilla extract

Preheat oven to 325 degrees. Line a 9x13 baking pan with parchment paper or aluminum foil. Spray with nonstick cooking spray.

In a medium bowl, combine pecans, flour, crushed Fiber One, baking powder, baking soda, and salt. Set aside.

In a small bowl, combine canola oil, applesauce, brown sugar, and honey. Add eggs, root-beer concentrate, and vanilla extract. Stir until ingredients are well blended.

Pour into flour mixture. Stir until well blended. Pour mixture into pan.

Bake for 20-25 minutes. Cool. Cut and serve.

Yield: **24 bars**

Nutrition Facts per Serving
Calories: 80, Fat calories: 45, Total fat: 5 g, Saturated fat: 0 g, Cholesterol: 15 mg, Sodium: 15 mg, Total carbohydrates: 10 g, Dietary fiber: 1 g, Sugar: 6 g, Protein: 1 g

Traditional Medium Root-Beer Float Nutrition Facts per Serving
Calories: 520, Total fat: 23 g, Sodium: 275 mg, Total carbohydrates: 75 g

Mireille's Super-Fabulous Crispy Treats

The kid in all of us loves Rice Krispies treats. While puffed-rice cereal is low in fat, I wanted to punch up the fiber. I made this fun transition by using Fiber One Honey Clusters. My daughter Mireille loves these treats, and I promise you will as well.

Nonstick cooking spray
4 cups Fiber One Honey Clusters
2¾ cups miniature marshmallows

¾ cup dark chocolate chips
2½ tbsp. applesauce
2 tsp. vanilla extract

Line a 9x13 baking pan with parchment paper. Spray with non-stick cooking spray.

Place Fiber One Honey Clusters in a large bowl.

In a large bowl, microwave 2½ cups miniature marshmallows, dark chocolate chips, and applesauce for 1 minute. Stir. Microwave for 1 minute. Remove and stir.

Stir in vanilla. Pour over cereal and toss. Stir in ¼ cup miniature marshmallows.

Press mixture evenly into pan. Place in refrigerator for 1 hour. Cut and serve.

Yield: *24 treats*

Nutrition Facts per Serving
Calories: 80, Fat calories: 25, Total fat: 2.5 g, Saturated fat: 1.5 g, Cholesterol: 0 mg, Sodium: 45 mg, Total carbohydrates: 16 g, Dietary fiber: 3 g, Sugar: 8 g, Protein: 1 g

Traditional Rice Krispies Treats Nutrition Facts per Serving
Calories: 153, Total fat: 33 g, Total carbohydrates: less than 30 g

Skinny Dark-Chocolate Bacon Cupcakes

How is bacon a part of a skinny recipe? Hear me out. I stumbled upon the original version of this recipe online and made some very simple modifications, including reducing the bacon from 12 slices to 2. I continued by decreasing 2 cups sugar to 1 cup and adding 1 ¼ cups applesauce. I also replaced half the flour with almond flour. Finally, instead of frosting, I drizzled the cupcakes with melted dark chocolate. You will love this!

Nonstick cooking spray
1 cup all-purpose flour
1 cup almond flour
¾ cup unsweetened cocoa powder
1 cup sugar
2 tsp. baking soda
2 tsp. baking powder
½ tsp. salt

2 eggs
1 tsp. vanilla extract
1 cup cold coffee
1 cup low-fat buttermilk
1 ¼ cups applesauce
2 tbsp. canola oil
2 tbsp. dark chocolate chips
2 slices bacon, cooked and crumbled

Preheat oven to 375 degrees. Line 2 muffin pans with paper cupcake liners. Spray with non-stick cooking spray.

In a medium bowl, combine flour, almond flour, cocoa powder, sugar, baking soda, baking powder, and salt.

In a separate bowl, combine eggs, vanilla extract, coffee, buttermilk, applesauce, and canola oil. Pour liquid mixture into flour mixture. Beat for 1 minute.

Spoon batter into muffin cups. Bake for 20-25 minutes. Cool pans on a wire rack.

Microwave dark chocolate for 30-60 seconds until melted. Drizzle over cupcakes. Sprinkle bacon on cupcakes.

Yield: 24 cupcakes

Nutrition Facts per Serving
Calories: 140, Fat calories: 70, Total fat: 7 g, Saturated fat: 1 g, Cholesterol: 15 mg, Sodium: 190 mg, Total carbohydrates: 18 g, Dietary fiber: 2 g, Sugar: 11 g, Protein 4 g

Traditional Dark-Chocolate Bacon Cupcake Nutrition Facts per Serving
Calories: 318, Total fat: 6 g, Sodium: 431 mg, Total carbohydrates: 38 g

Skinny Sweet-Potato Cupcakes

This 100-calorie, vitamin-A-rich dessert features the Louisiana state vegetable—the sweet potato! How did I skinny it? I decreased the sugar to ¾ cup and the butter to 2 tbsp. whipped butter, greatly reducing carbs and calories. My kids love these cupcakes, and you will as well.

Nonstick cooking spray
4 sweet potatoes, cooked, peeled, and
   mashed
¾ cup sugar
6 large egg yolks, lightly beaten
⅛ tsp. salt

1 tsp. cinnamon
⅛ tsp. nutmeg
2 tbsp. whipped butter
½ cup unsweetened applesauce
12 oz. fat-free evaporated milk
2½ tsp. vanilla extract

Preheat oven to 350 degrees. Spray a muffin pan with nonstick cooking spray.

In a large bowl, combine sweet potatoes, sugar, egg yolks, salt, cinnamon, nutmeg, whipped butter, applesauce, evaporated milk, and vanilla. Beat with hand mixer on lowest speed for 1 minute.

Divide filling among muffin cups. Bake for 50-65 minutes. Serve.

Yield: 18 cupcakes

Nutrition Facts per Serving
Calories: 100, Fat calories: 26, Total fat: 2.5 g, Saturated fat: 1 g, Cholesterol: 65 mg, Sodium: 75 mg, Total carbohydrates: 18 g, Dietary fiber: 1 g, Sugar: 13 g, Protein: 3 g

Traditional Sweet-Potato Tart Nutrition Facts per Serving
Calories: 340, Total fat: 17 g, Cholesterol: 40 mg, Sodium: 240 mg, Total carbohydrates: 44 g

SWeet-potato Chocolate-Chip Cookies

We can all remember the first time we smelled cookies baking in the oven. Welcome that aroma into your Skinny Louisiana kitchen with these treats. Replacing the butter in the traditional chocolate-chip cookie recipe with a mashed sweet potato makes that possible! I promise, these cookies will not disappoint.

½ cup quick-cooking oats
¼ cup peanut butter
1 egg
2 tbsp. honey
1 tbsp. vanilla extract
½ tsp. cinnamon

½ tsp. baking soda
½ tsp. baking powder
Dash of salt
1 sweet potato, peeled, cooked, and
   mashed
½ cup dark chocolate chips

Preheat oven to 350 degrees. Line a baking sheet with parchment paper or aluminum foil.

In a large bowl, combine oats, peanut butter, egg, honey, vanilla, cinnamon, baking soda, baking powder, and salt. Beat for 1 minute.

Stir in sweet potato. Beat for 30 seconds.

Stir in dark chocolate chips. Drop dough by the tablespoonful onto baking sheet. Bake for 15-20 minutes. Cool.

Yield: 24 cookies

Nutrition Facts per Serving
Calories: 60, Fat calories: 30, Total fat: 3 g, Saturated fat: 1.5 g, Cholesterol: 0 mg, Sodium: 35 mg, Total carbohydrates: 7 g, Dietary fiber: less than 1 g, Sugar: 4 g, Protein: 1 g

Subway Chocolate-Chip Cookie Nutrition Facts per Serving
Calories: 220, Total fat: 10 g, Sodium: 130 mg, Total carbohydrates: 30 g

SKiNNy PuMPKiN-PraLiNe Bread PuddiNg

Bread pudding is a must-have dessert in my family. Don't believe me? My wedding desserts were the traditional wedding cake and chocolate groom's cake, but we added a third: bread pudding! What better dessert to showcase on the Thanksgiving table than this pumpkin-praline bread pudding?

Nonstick cooking spray

1 loaf day-old French bread, torn into small pieces

2 cups fat-free half-and-half

1 can (10 oz.) pumpkin puree

¾ cup applesauce

¾ cup sugar

4 eggs

1 tbsp. vanilla extract

1 tbsp. pumpkin pie spice

TOPPING

½ cup applesauce

½ cup fat-free half-and-half

½ cup honey

½ cup chopped pecans

Preheat oven to 350 degrees. Spray a 9x13 baking pan with nonstick cooking spray. Add torn bread pieces to baking pan.

In a large bowl, combine half-and-half, pumpkin puree, applesauce, sugar, eggs, vanilla, and pumpkin pie spice. Beat for 1 minute.

Pour mixture over bread. Bake for 50-60 minutes.

While bread pudding is baking, make praline topping. In a small saucepan over medium-low heat, combine applesauce, half-and-half, and honey. Bring to a boil.

Reduce heat to low. Stir in pecans. Simmer for 3 minutes.

Pour over bread pudding. Serve.

Yield: 16 servings

Nutrition Facts per Serving
Calories: 190, Fat calories: 40, Total fat: 4.5 g, Saturated fat: 1 g, Cholesterol: 50 mg, Sodium: 135 mg, Total carbohydrates: 34 g, Dietary fiber: 2 g, Sugar: 23 g, Protein: 5 g

Traditional Pumpkin-Praline Bread Pudding Nutrition Facts per Serving
Calories: 450, Total fat: 21 g, Cholesterol: 100 mg, Sodium: 470 mg, Total carbohydrates: 58 g

Skinny Cream-Cheese Chocolate-Chip Bread Pudding

I combined the amazing flavors of chocolate and bread pudding in this health-conscious creation. How did I skinny it? I switched over to reduced-fat croissant dough and light cream cheese to lower fat, and I replaced most of the sugar with applesauce to decrease calories.

Nonstick cooking spray
6 reduced-fat croissant dough
8 oz. light cream cheese
½ cup dark chocolate chips
4 eggs
4 egg whites or ½ cup Egg Beaters

1 cup applesauce
½ cup sugar
2 tbsp. vanilla extract
½ tsp. salt
3 cups fat-free half-and-half

Spray a 9x13 baking pan with nonstick cooking spray.

Slice croissant doughs into ½-inch slices. Cut cream cheese into small pieces. In a small bowl, combine croissants, cream cheese, and dark chocolate chips. Pour mixture into baking pan.

In a large bowl, combine eggs, egg whites (or Egg Beaters), applesauce, sugar, vanilla extract, and salt. Beat for 2 minutes.

Add half-and-half. Beat for 1 minute.

Pour mixture over croissant mixture. Cover and chill for 1 hour or longer.

Preheat oven to 350 degrees. Bake for 50-60 minutes or until bread pudding is golden brown.

Remove pan from oven and let stand for 10 minutes before serving.

Yield: 16 servings

Nutrition Facts per Serving
Calories: 190, Fat calories: 80, Total fat: 9 g, Saturated fat: 4.5 g, Cholesterol: 60 mg, Sodium: 310 mg, Total carbohydrates: 23 g, Dietary fiber: 1 g, Sugar: 15 g, Protein: 6 g

Carrabba's Triple Chocolate Bread Pudding Nutrition Facts per Serving
Calories: 1,514, Total fat: 104 g, Cholesterol: 269 mg, Sodium: 614 mg, Total carbohydrates: 121 g

SKiNNY KiNG Cake Bread PUddiNG

From the time I was a little girl in Houma, I loved Mardi Gras "pawades," but more importantly, I loved king cake. And while my passion for this Carnival treat continues, I'm not wild about all the calories, fat, and carbs that come with it. This version combines the delicious flavors of a traditional king cake with the creaminess of bread pudding. I simply reduced the sugar in both the cake and toppings, and while I used bread, remember this is Mardi Gras!

1 loaf French bread, cut into pieces
4 eggs
1 cup Egg Beaters
2 cups fat-free half-and-half
2 cups 2 percent milk
1½ cups sugar
1 tsp. almond extract
1 tbsp. vanilla extract

GLAZE
½ cup powdered sugar
4 tbsp. 2 percent milk
1½ tsp. almond extract

MARDI GRAS SUGAR
3 tbsp. sugar
Yellow food coloring
Green food coloring
Purple food coloring

Preheat oven to 350 degrees. Place bread pieces in a 9x13 baking pan.

In a large bowl, combine eggs, Egg Beaters, half-and-half, milk, sugar, almond extract, and vanilla extract. Whisk until blended. Gently pour mixture over bread.

Let bread mixture stand for 30 minutes. Flip bread to make sure pieces are soaked with milk mixture.

Bake for 30-40 minutes or until mixture is set in center. Cool.

To prepare glaze, in a small bowl, combine sugar, milk, and almond extract.

To prepare Mardi Gras Sugar, in 3 zip-top bags, place 1 tbsp. sugar each. Add food coloring to each bag, using a different color for each. Shake.

Pour glaze over prepared bread pudding. Sprinkle with colored sugars.

Yield: *12 servings*

Nutrition Facts per Serving

Calories: 130, Fat calories: 25, Total fat: 2.5 g, Saturated fat: 1 g, Cholesterol: 50 mg, Sodium: 160 mg, Total carbohydrates: 19 g, Dietary fiber: 0 g, Sugar: 10 g, Protein: 6 g

Traditional Bread Pudding Nutrition Facts per Serving

Calories: 306, Total fat: 9.4 g, Sodium: 472 mg, Total carbohydrates: 46 g

INdeX